THE **CONNECTION**

CONNECTION

THE
CONNECTION

How al Qaeda's Collaboration
with Saddam Hussein
Has Endangered America

STEPHEN F. HAYES

HarperCollins*Publishers*

HarperCollins books may be purchased for educational, business, or sales promotional use. For information, please write: Special Markets Department, HarperCollins Publishers Inc., 10 East 53rd Street, New York, NY 10022.

FIRST EDITION

Designed by Elliott Beard

Printed on acid-free paper

Library of Congress Cataloging-in-Publication Data is available upon request.

ISBN 0-06-074673-4

04 05 06 07 08 v/RRD 10 9 8 7 6 5 4 3 2 1

To Sergeant First Class Curtis "Paco" Mancini
and the many heroes of the War on Terror

"Because the job is never done"

CONTENTS

PREFACE

This book is the product of more than two years of covering the War on Terror and Iraq for the *Weekly Standard*. That reporting includes several trips to the Middle East; three to Iraq. It draws on sources built in that time and includes hundreds of interviews with former Iraqi military officers; Iraqi immigrants to the United States; senior officials in the new Iraqi government, in Europe, and in the Middle East; current and former U.S. intelligence officials; soldiers and officers in the U.S. military; and senior policy makers in both the Clinton and Bush administrations.

Wherever possible, I identify my sources by name. The sensitive nature of some of the information in this book makes it impossible to do so in every case.

Much of the information in this book comes from "open sources," those readily available to anyone with patience and a computer. The U.S. intelligence community has long been skeptical of open-source reporting. That is changing. John C. Gannon, then chairman of the National Intelligence Council, addressed these changes in an October 6, 2000, speech. Open-source reporting, he said, "is more important than ever in the post–Cold War world . . . It is indispensable to the production of authoritative analysis. It increasingly contains the best information to answer our most important questions." These open sources include unclassified government reports, court documents, and news media reports.

Whenever an open source includes or corroborates information I have obtained through unnamed or secret sources, I cite the open source.

Some of the information in this book comes from highly classified documents. I have taken great care to protect the sources and methods that contributed to the production of those documents. One of these, a memo from the undersecretary of defense for policy, Douglas J. Feith, to the Senate Intelligence Committee, was reviewed by a panel of four intelligence experts who served both Republicans and Democrats to ensure that no information that could jeopardize national security was compromised.

The Feith memo, as it has become known, was requested of the Pentagon by the Senate Intelligence Committee. Dated October 27, 2003, it expanded on testimony Mr. Feith provided to the committee on the relationship between Iraq and al Qaeda and contained a "classified annex" that detailed the collaboration. The intelligence in the memo came from a variety of sources: detainee debriefings, communications intercepts, open sources, raw intelligence reports, and finished products of the Central Intelligence Agency, National Security Agency, and Federal Bureau of Investigation.

I obtained the document in the fall of 2003 and included sections of it in an article I wrote for the *Weekly Standard* called "Case Closed," released online on November 14, 2003.

The day after the story was published, the Pentagon released a statement. "News reports that the Defense Department recently confirmed new information with respect to contacts between al Qaeda and Iraq in a letter to the Senate Intelligence Committee are inaccurate." The Pentagon statement was classic Washington "nondenial denial." It specified neither the allegedly "inaccurate" news reports nor the alleged inaccuracies.

More worrisome, the Pentagon statement was itself inaccurate. Among other things, the statement maintained that the relevant section "was not an analysis of the substantive issue of the relationship between Iraq and al Qaeda, and it drew no conclusions." The language of the Feith memo plainly contradicts this assertion. The annex is called "Summary of Body of Intelligence Reporting on Iraq–al Qaeda Contacts (1990–2003)." It contains passages in normal typeface and in bold. A note at the bottom of the first page reads: "All bolded sentences contain information from intelligence reporting. Unbolded sentences represent comments/analyses." The opening paragraph of the Feith memo contains this conclusion: "The substantial body of intelligence reporting—for over a decade—from a variety of sources—reflects a pattern of Iraqi support for al Qaeda's activities."

Reporters seized on the Pentagon press release and largely ignored the findings of the Feith memo. The *Washington Post* story about the Feith memo focused as much on the alleged leak of the document as on the document itself. So did an article in the *New York Times,* written nearly a week after the memo was brought to light. Several prominent journalists seemed far more interested in discrediting the *Weekly Standard* article—

and by extension the Feith memo—than they were in reporting and analyzing its contents. Their attempts were error-filled and in some cases misleading.

Newsweek reporters Michael Isikoff and Mark Hosenball dismissed the *Weekly Standard* article as "hype" and concluded that the "tangled tale of the memo suggests that the case of whether there has been Iraq–al Qaeda complicity is far from closed." The authors argued that "the Pentagon memo pointedly omits any reference to the interrogations of a host of other high-level al Qaeda and Iraqi detainees—including such notables as Khalid Sheikh Mohammed, Ramzi bin al Shibh, Abu Zubaydah and [Faruq Hijazi]."

In fact, the Feith memo included summaries of the debriefings of both Abu Zubaydah and Faruq Hijazi. The interrogations were not included in the *Weekly Standard* article for space reasons; the Feith memo was sixteen pages long.

The *Newsweek* writers further claimed that the *Weekly Standard* article overlooked the fact that "the Pentagon memo itself concedes that much of the recent reporting about Iraq–al Qaeda ties is 'conflicting.'" Their indictment is exactly backward. The Feith memo made no such claim. The *Weekly Standard* article did.

Daniel Benjamin, the former head of counterterrorism on the National Security Council in the Clinton White House, also sought to discredit the article. In an article published in *Slate* on December 9, 2003, he wrote: "Not surprisingly, none of the reports in the Feith memo mention the aversion that the Baathist[s] and jihadists felt for one another." In fact, the Feith memo makes four separate and specific references to these religious and ideological differences.

The controversy heated up again in January. Vice President Dick Cheney was interviewed on January 9, 2004, by M. E. Sprengelmeyer of the *Rocky Mountain News*. The reporter asked Cheney if soldiers in Iraq had been "misled" about connections between Iraq and al Qaeda. "One place you ought to look is an article that Stephen Hayes did in the *Weekly Standard* here a few weeks ago. It goes through and lays out in some detail, based on an assessment that was done by the Department of Defense and was forwarded to the Senate Intelligence Committee some weeks ago. That's your best source of information."

Senator Carl Levin, a Democrat from Michigan, asked CIA director George Tenet about the Feith memo during a session of the Senate Intelligence Committee on February 24, 2004. "Last November the *Weekly Standard* published excerpts from an alleged classified document that was prepared under Secretary of Defense Feith's leadership. It was dated October 27, 2003. This document was sent to the Senate Intelligence Committee. It alleged an operational relationship between Iraq and the al Qaeda terrorist organization. It's become quite a cause célèbre. Did the Department of Defense consult with the CIA before sending that document to the Senate Intelligence Committee?"

Tenet could not provide an answer, so Levin asked him again on March 9, 2004, in an appearance before the Senate Armed Services Committee. "Senator, we did not clear that document," said Tenet. Pentagon officials strenuously disagree. The intelligence reporting included in the document had a classification status known to the intelligence community as ORCON. That status requires any recipient of the intelligence to consult the agency from which the intelligence originates before sharing it with any other agency. Defense Department officials insist that they undertook such consultations with the CIA. They say Tenet may have simply been unaware of the vetting because such discussions usually involve low-level staffers.

"We did not agree with the way the data was characterized in that document," Tenet said, adding that the CIA submitted its own version of the Feith memo to the intelligence committee.

That CIA analysts would have different analyses of the intelligence in the Pentagon document is hardly surprising. The Pentagon unit that undertook the alternative analysis did so in part because the original CIA analysis of the Iraq–al Qaeda relationship was determined to be myopic and incomplete. That said, a significant number of the items included in the Feith memo come from finished CIA products. I have endeavored here to include as much descriptive information as possible about the intelligence and its source.

It may turn out that some of the reporting in the memo will not check out under further scrutiny. Indeed, the analysis of the document in these pages raises several questions about the plausibility of some specific reports.

Still, much of the information is detailed, conclusive, and corroborated by multiple sources. And nothing has yet proven false. It comes from foreign and domestic intelligence agencies, including the Federal Bureau of Investigation, the Central Intelligence Agency, the National Security Agency, and the Defense Intelligence Agency.

INTRODUCTION

**The evidence now shows clearly that Saddam did
not want to work with Osama bin Laden at all,
much less give him weapons of mass destruction.**

—Former Vice President Al Gore

**Clearly the al Qaeda connection was hyped and
exaggerated, in my view.**

—Senator Dianne Feinstein,
Democrat from California

**There is no credible evidence that Iraq actively
aided al Qaeda.**

—Report published by the Carnegie Endowment
for International Peace

**There's absolutely no evidence that Iraq was
supporting al Qaeda, ever.**

—Richard Clarke, former counterterrorism official
under Bill Clinton and George W. Bush

Welcome to the new conventional wisdom.

National network anchors report that there is "no link" between Iraq and al Qaeda, and syndicated columnists dismiss the
connection as "fictional." Politicians who oppose President

Bush point to the connection as an example of his administration's duplicity, while those who support him generally remain silent. On the Washington, D.C., cocktail party circuit the mere mention of Iraq–al Qaeda ties elicits laughter, even derision.

This conventional wisdom is comforting, to be sure. But it's also wrong.

No two events have shaped the Bush presidency as much as the September 11 terrorist attacks and the war in Iraq. In the former, on a crisp fall morning, four commercial planes slammed into New York City's World Trade Center, the Pentagon, and a remote field in Pennsylvania, killing hundreds of innocent civilians instantly. Within hours, the Twin Towers collapsed, killing thousands more. In the latter, a determined American military in the spring of 2003 easily rolled back an army controlled by one of the world's most ruthless dictators. Within months, Saddam Hussein was found cowering inside a small dirt hole, and images of his tongue being prodded like a barn animal's were broadcast worldwide, showing a ravaged country and the rest of the world that he would no longer be able to rape, torture, or massacre thousands.

As much as those two events crystallized America's vulnerability and strength, they are commonly viewed as separate and discrete, neither having to do with the other. "I believe that to talk about Iraq as the center of antiterror efforts is to try to lose the focus on Osama bin Laden and al Qaeda and the global efforts that we need to undertake," said Senator John Kerry, who nonetheless voted to authorize the war. The Bush administration's conduct of that war, Kerry argues, has made us less safe: "The global war on terrorism has actually been set back."

Kerry is not alone in making that argument. To great fanfare and much media adulation, former Bush administration counterterrorism official Richard Clarke offered a similar assessment in the spring of 2004. Clarke faulted President Bush for ignoring warnings about the al Qaeda threat before the September 11 attacks and savaged his administration for going to war in Iraq. "By invading Iraq, the President of the United States has greatly undermined the war on terror."

If John Kerry and the cognoscenti believe that Saddam Hussein's Iraq was a needless distraction from the War on Terror, the terrorists do not. For more than a decade, Osama bin Laden cited the Gulf War and U.S. troop presence on "sacred land" as the reason for his attacks. Al Qaeda pointed to the more recent war in Iraq to explain attacks in Turkey, Saudi Arabia, the Philippines, and Spain—U.S. allies in that war.

More directly, the claim that the Iraq War undermined the War on Terror rests on a perilous presumption: Saddam Hussein did not and would not support radical Islamic terrorists like Osama bin Laden. That presumption is also wrong.

Among the many lessons of the September 11 attacks is one that Americans and their leaders should have learned years earlier. Enemies who threaten to kill U.S. citizens must be taken seriously. Enemies who make good on those threats must be eliminated.

Osama bin Laden warned America several times that his terrorists would commit mass murder in the name of Islam. Six people died and more than one thousand were injured in the first World Trade Center attack in 1993. Two hundred fifty-seven people died and more than five thousand were injured in the twin al Qaeda bombings at U.S. embassies in Kenya and Tanzania in 1998. Seventeen U.S. sailors were killed when the USS *Cole* was bombed by al Qaeda terrorists in Yemen in 2000. After each of these attacks, bin Laden promised more carnage. And after each of these attacks, his terrorist network delivered.

Bin Laden was not the only foe who threatened to kill Americans. Beginning with his defeat in the first Gulf War, Saddam Hussein insisted for more than a decade that the conflict was only a temporary setback in his continuing war against America. His threats were direct and terrifying.

Saddam, too, attempted to make good on those threats. In 1991, he sent intelligence agents throughout the world on missions to strike at U.S. and Western targets. In 1993, he sent a team of intelligence assets to Kuwait City to assassinate his nemesis, George H. W. Bush. In 1998, he authorized a plan to blow up a building that housed U.S. government–funded broadcasts in Prague, Czech Republic.

Then came September 11.

Suddenly, the difference between bin Laden and Saddam—al Qaeda attacks often succeeded and known Iraqi attacks usually failed—mattered far less than their common, oft-stated goal: killing Americans.

In the days after the attacks, world leaders expressed sympathy and solidarity with Americans. The list of well-wishers included longtime enemies such as Cuba's Fidel Castro, Libya's Moammar Khadafi, and the ruling clerics in Iran.

There was only one exception: Saddam Hussein.

As distraught relatives searched for missing loved ones near

Ground Zero, the Iraqi regime openly celebrated. To the strains of triumphant, nationalistic music, Iraq's state-run television network replayed the spectacular images of the two airplanes crashing into the World Trade Center. And as the Twin Towers collapsed, the opening lyrics of one song—"Down with America"—took on a grim literal meaning. One Iraqi government newspaper declared: "The great power that once sowed terror throughout the world was yesterday terrified, thrown into panic and humiliated."

Most stunning, Saddam Hussein himself said that Americans got what they deserved. "Those who do not want to harvest evil should not plant evil," he said. "The American Cowboys are reaping the fruit of their crimes against humanity."

There is no proof that the Iraqi regime had any operational involvement in the September 11 attacks. And it should go without saying that the U.S. government cannot run around the world toppling dictators simply because they have threatened Americans. But potential collaboration between Osama bin Laden and Saddam Hussein presented a unique threat.

In the days after the September 11 attacks, Americans were told that the horror of that day was the result of a failure to "connect the dots."

A 1995 plot to crash an airplane into the CIA. A 1999 Congressional Research Service report about the prospect of hijacked airlines packed with bombs used as weapons. A high level of unspecific intelligence "chatter" in the summer of 2001. An internal FBI field office memo marked "routine" by its author about suspicious Middle Eastern men in Phoenix flight schools. A CIA briefing that mentions possible al Qaeda hijacking.

These dots and others were not connected. Politicians and journalists avoided pointing fingers for eight months. Then the public learned about that last dot. On August 6, 2001, President Bush received his daily intelligence briefing at his ranch in Texas. Among several other items was one that stood out in retrospect: al Qaeda wanted to attack the United States, and hijacking airplanes was one of the possible means.

The hushed whispers of blame that had been circulating in the nation's capital suddenly burst out into the open.

"9/11 BOMBSHELL: BUSH KNEW!" blared the front page of the *New York Post* on May 16, 2002.

Later that day, Hillary Clinton took to the floor of the Senate with a copy of the newspaper in hand. "I am simply here today on the floor of this hallowed chamber to seek answers to the questions being asked by my constituents, questions raised by one of our newspapers in New York, with the headline 'Bush Knew.' The president knew what?" Her constituents were not looking to place blame, she disingenuously claimed, but they deserved answers "to that and many other questions."

Dick Gephardt was less subtle. At a May 16, 2002, press conference, he invoked an infamous Watergate-era formulation: "What we have to do now is find out what the president—what the White House—knew about the events leading up to 9/11, when they knew it and, most importantly, what was done about it."

It was incendiary rhetoric. The Democrats quickly backed off. But even as they tempered their critique, they intensified their calls for an independent investigation.

Such an inquiry was appropriate. The attacks of September 11 had plainly been the result of a massive intelligence failure.

The goal of such an inquiry would be to answer a question asked by journalists, the family members of victims, and all Americans: How could our intelligence community have missed the signs of the impending attack?

Never again, went the promise, would there be such a failure to "connect the dots." This pledge more than anything else explains the war in Iraq.

The Bush administration made a three-part case for war: Saddam Hussein's brutality against his fellow Iraqis; the failure of the Iraqi regime to account for its weapons of mass destruction; and the most controversial of the three casus belli: Iraq's connections with Osama bin Laden and al Qaeda.

The first two parts of that case were not in serious dispute. No one denied Saddam's mass slaughter of Iraqis, and virtually every intelligence agency in the world believed that his regime possessed weapons of mass destruction. The case on Iraq's connection to al Qaeda was more circumstantial. It would require people to connect the dots.

But by the time the Iraq War began, the evidence of Iraqi links to al Qaeda went well beyond a few dots. It was a veritable constellation.

An important participant in the first al Qaeda attack on American soil, the 1993 bombing of the World Trade Center, had been given safe haven in Iraq. Both bin Laden and Saddam had repeatedly voiced their desire to kill Americans. CIA director George Tenet reported at least eight meetings between high-level Iraqi intelligence officials and senior al Qaeda terrorists. At least twice, the deputy director of Iraqi intelligence met bin Laden personally. In its 1998 indictment of bin Laden, the Clinton administration cited an "understanding" between

Iraq and al Qaeda whereby bin Laden agreed not to agitate against the Iraqi regime in exchange for help on "weapons development." Fresh intelligence indicated that Iraq had provided training to al Qaeda terrorists on poisons and gases. Senior al Qaeda associates were operating openly in Baghdad before the war.

Critics of the Bush administration, including many experts and politicians who once warned about Iraq–al Qaeda connections, now conveniently shrug off this evidence. The president doesn't have that luxury.

One of the most oft-repeated clichés to come out of the attacks on the Pentagon and the World Trade Center is that "September 11 changed everything." It's half right. September 11 changed little for the terrorists. They had been at war with the United States for a decade, and the September 11 attacks were simply a more successful battle in a much longer campaign.

What changed, then, was America's response to terror. The battle was joined. The war would involve more than warnings, more than démarches, more than back-channel diplomacy, more than empty threats. Terrorists and the states that sponsor them would be eliminated.

Saddam Hussein was one of those terrorists, and he ran one of those states. His regime harbored, financed, supported, and armed terrorists determined to kill Americans.

He was, in the words of one of his own generals, "the father and grandfather of terrorists."

THE **CONNECTION**

CHAPTER ONE

CASE OPEN:
WHO IS AHMED HIKMAT SHAKIR?

In August 2000, Ahmed Hikmat Shakir, a thirty-seven-year-old Iraqi, quietly began his job as a "greeter" at the Kuala Lumpur International Airport in Malaysia. The job, a common one in Southeast Asia and the Middle East, normally involves little more than welcoming visiting dignitaries and making certain that they move smoothly through the laborious entry process.

But Shakir was not a typical greeter. Although he was nominally employed by Malaysian Airlines, he had told associates he had been hired by a contact in the Iraqi embassy. More important, it was his embassy contact, not his employer, who told him when to report and when to take days off. So when the Iraqi embassy contact instructed him to report to work on January 5, 2000, Shakir dutifully obliged. His assignment that day would later make him the subject of an international manhunt and a suspect in the worst single act of terrorism on American soil.

The events of that day and those that followed provide the government's strongest suggestion that Saddam and al Qaeda may have worked together on September 11. The evidence is far from conclusive, but it cannot be dismissed. Those events are also an unfortunate example of the difficulty of maintaining effective liaison relationships between American and foreign intelligence services, and of how, even in the months following the worst intelligence failure in American history, dangerous terrorists were allowed to walk away from their cramped holding cells as free men.

In late December 1999, the Central Intelligence Agency, the National Security Agency, and the State Department all received intelligence about a meeting of al Qaeda–associated terrorists to take place in Malaysia in early January of the next year. The NSA had intercepted communications from individuals tied to the 1998 al Qaeda attacks on U.S. embassies in Kenya and Tanzania. Although the information was incomplete, the intercepts picked up three first names: Khalid, Nawaf, and Salem.

The CIA, on high alert for potential attacks on millennium celebrations, immediately sent word to operatives around the world to track the would-be terrorists. On December 31, 1999, CIA officials in Pakistan cabled to headquarters that they "were following the situation." Nawaf was in Pakistan and Khalid was in Yemen. The CIA determined that they planned to meet in Kuala Lumpur, Malaysia, arriving on January 4, 2000, and established an operation—to be conducted jointly with Malaysian intelligence—to monitor the comings and goings of the men. CIA officials assumed the meeting was called to plan attacks in Southeast Asia.

That same day, the CIA obtained a photocopy of the passport belonging to one of the suspected participants, Khalid al Mihdhar. Although al Mihdhar, a Saudi citizen, was known to have connections to al Qaeda and the Yemeni mujahideen, he was not yet on any terrorist watch lists on April 7, 1999, when the U.S. consulate in Jidda, Saudi Arabia, had given him a one-year visa granting him multiple-entry privilege to the United States.

The intelligence on Nawaf al Hazmi, at that point known only by his first name, was sketchier. The CIA determined that he was scheduled to leave Karachi, Pakistan, for Malaysia on January 4, 2000. In fact, he had departed two days earlier.

On January 5, 2000, officials at CIA headquarters in Langley, Virginia, sent a dispatch to operatives around the world that "we need to continue the effort to identify these travelers and their activities . . . to determine if there is any true threat posed." Information about the meeting was included in the al Qaeda–related intelligence given to the most senior officials in the U.S. government. On at least two occasions, the director of the CIA's al Qaeda unit gave briefings to his superiors about the meeting.

Khalid al Mihdhar, a thin, dark-haired man with a slightly crooked face, arrived at the Kuala Lumpur International Airport on January 5. The airport is an architectural wonder—a glass-enclosed tribute to modernity that attracts even tourists who arrive elsewhere in the Malaysian capital. The marble floors are buffed constantly, producing a surface so shiny, it's possible to catch a glimpse of yourself simply by looking down. Round white beams shoot like three-dimensional spiderwebs from the floor to the unfinished ceiling, and Western stores such as the Tie Rack line the halls of the main terminal.

Ahmed Hikmat Shakir, the Iraqi greeter, met al Mihdhar shortly after he deplaned and escorted him through the bu-

4 STEPHEN F. HAYES

reaucratic entry procedures. Malaysian authorities photographed the arrival.

When they had finished the paperwork, Shakir walked al Mihdhar to a waiting car, much as any facilitator would. But then, rather than bidding his VIP good-bye and returning to work, Shakir jumped in the car and accompanied al Mihdhar to a condominium owned by Yazid Sufaat, an American-educated al Qaeda associate, where he was once again photographed by Malaysian intelligence. The Kuala Lumpur condo would serve as the site of a three-day meeting that the CIA later concluded was the main planning session for the October 12, 2000, bombing of the USS *Cole* and for the attacks of September 11, 2001. It is not yet known whether Shakir took an active part in the meeting, but he was certainly in fast company. The FBI believes as many as nine top al Qaeda terrorists attended the meeting, including Ramzi bin al Shibh, who later boasted to a journalist of his role as "coordinator of the Holy Tuesday operation"—the September 11 attacks.

The meeting ended on January 8, 2000, when three of the participants—Khalid al Mihdhar, Nawaf al Hazmi, and Khallad bin Attash—left Kuala Lumpur for Bangkok, Thailand. Of the three, the CIA was still able to identify only al Mihdhar by his full name. CIA officials in Kuala Lumpur notified their counterparts in Thailand and asked them to pick up the surveillance, and the agency's Langley, Virginia, headquarters sent an urgent cable the next day with the same instructions. These messages came too late; the al Qaeda suspects had disappeared into the busy streets of Bangkok.

Shakir, the Iraqi greeter, reported to work at the Kuala

Lumpur International Airport on January 9 and 10. He never showed up again.

On January 12, 2000, the chief of the CIA's al Qaeda unit briefed his bosses about the Kuala Lumpur meeting. The official, apparently unaware that the meeting had broken up four days earlier, reported erroneously that the surveillance in Kuala Lumpur was continuing. Three days later, unbeknownst to U.S. officials, al Hazmi and al Mihdhar slipped onto a United Airlines flight from Bangkok to Los Angeles.

On September 11, 2001, Nawaf al Hazmi and his brother Salem, along with Khalid al Mihdhar, hijacked American Airlines flight 77. At 9:38 A.M., the airplane struck the Pentagon.

Six days later, authorities in Qatar arrested Shakir in Doha, the nation's capital, where he had been working as a mid-level employee at Qatar's Ministry of Religious Development. The CIA had learned Shakir's identity, but not his whereabouts, after the Kuala Lumpur meeting ended. In the short time since the 9/11 attacks, the FBI had identified al Hazmi and al Mihdhar as two of the hijackers and placed Shakir at the meeting in Malaysia.

Shakir's presence at the gathering in Kuala Lumpur wasn't the only thing that piqued investigators' interest in him. According to CIA reporting, authorities found both on his person and in his Doha apartment, a stunning collection of information on some very dangerous characters. The terrorists in touch with Shakir had both strong ties to al Qaeda and indirect links to the former regime in Iraq. Several of them had been involved in bloody attacks on Americans dating back to the early 1990s. The stash wasn't a complete surprise. The CIA had previous reporting that Shakir had received at least one phone call from the planning headquarters for the 1993 bombing of the World Trade Center.

Among Shakir's contacts were Zahid Sheikh Mohammed, the brother of September 11 mastermind Khalid Sheikh Mohammed; Musab Yasin, the brother of 1993 World Trade Center bomber Abdul Rahman Yasin, who was harbored and supported by the Iraqi regime for a decade after that attack; and Ibrahim Ahmad Suleiman, a U.S. citizen born in Kuwait, whose fingerprints were found on the bomb-making manuals authorities found after the 1993 WTC attack.

One contact stood out as a special indicator of Shakir's standing with al Qaeda: an old telephone number for Mamdouh Mahmud Salim, whose roots are suggested by his nom de guerre, Abu Hajer al Iraqi. The number reached a desk at Taba Investments, perhaps the best-known of Osama bin Laden's al Qaeda front companies. Abu Hajer, a founding member of al Qaeda, was described by another senior al Qaeda operative as Osama bin Laden's "best friend."

The preceding information reflects the consensus of the U.S. intelligence community. Virtually no one disputes the details. What happened next, however, and what it all means remain a source of intense debate inside the halls of U.S. intelligence agencies.

Despite Shakir's direct connections with several of the world's most dangerous terrorists, the Qatari government released him from custody. On October 21, 2001, he boarded a plane for Baghdad. But he didn't arrive there: he was detained at his connection in Amman by Jordanian intelligence. Immediately following his capture, according to U.S. officials familiar with the intelligence on Shakir, the Iraqi government began exerting pressure on the Jordanians to release him. Just how much pressure depends on whom you ask.

Some U.S. intelligence officials, primarily at the CIA, believe that Iraq's demand for Shakir's release was pro forma, no different from the requests governments regularly make on behalf of citizens detained by a foreign government. Others inside the CIA and in the national security hierarchy disagree. These officials point to the flurry of phone calls, diplomatic cables, and personal appeals from the Iraqi government to the Jordanians and contend that the reaction was anything but typical. This concern, they say, reflected an interest in Shakir at the highest levels of Saddam Hussein's regime.

Curiously, the Iraqi regime was not the only source of pressure for the Jordanian government. Within days of Shakir's capture, and before it had been publicly reported, the Amman-based office of Amnesty International sent a letter to Jordan's interior minister demanding an explanation of Shakir's detention. "It appears that his arrest may have been in connection with suspicions on the part of the Jordanian authorities relating to visits he had made to Pakistan, Yemen, and Malaysia," read a subsequent Amnesty International report, which also expressed concern that Shakir was "held in incommunicado detention for several weeks before being allowed access to a lawyer" and that "he had lost weight during his detention and appeared to be traumatized."

While in custody, Shakir was questioned first by the Jordanians and then by the CIA. The CIA officials who talked to Shakir reported that he was generally uncooperative. But even in refusing to talk, he provided some important information: the interrogators concluded that his evasive answers reflected counterinterrogation techniques so sophisticated that they likely had been learned from a government intelligence service. Shakir's nationality, his contacts with the Iraqi embassy in Malaysia, and the keen interest of Baghdad in his case make Iraq the most likely candidate.

But there are elements to Shakir's story that have left some at the CIA skeptical of his involvement with Iraqi intelligence. U.S. officials know the identity of his contact at the Iraqi embassy in Kuala Lumpur. Iraqi embassies were often heavily populated by intelligence officers, which in some cases account for more than half of all embassy employees. The CIA, which often had a good idea of which embassy employees were conducting official business and which ones were acting on behalf of Iraqi intelligence, had not previously identified Shakir's contact as an intelligence officer. Further, Saddam usually assigned his intelligence agents to high-ranking diplomatic posts, and U.S. intelligence officials agree that Shakir's contact was relatively low-ranking.

Did CIA officials overlook his potential connections to Iraqi intelligence because his position didn't fit its reporting on the practices of Iraqi intelligence officials in embassies throughout the world? It's possible. Some CIA officials would later discount Shakir's alleged connections to Iraqi intelligence, citing his contact's low rank as a primary reason.

Others at the CIA, the Pentagon, and the National Security Council disagree. Given the obvious gaps in the American government's knowledge about Iraqi intelligence, they contend, it would be dangerously rigid thinking to assume that every Iraqi agent—with no exception—occupied a high-profile embassy position. And even if this is consistently true of intelligence operatives in Iraq embassies, how can we be certain that every Iraqi embassy employee in Malaysia fits that same pattern?

In any case, Jordanian intelligence concluded not only that Shakir's embassy contact was likely from Iraqi intelligence, but that Shakir himself was working on behalf of the Iraqi Intelligence Service (IIS)—and playing an important role.

So the Jordanians—who cooperated so extensively with U.S. intelligence after September 11 that CIA director George Tenet would later praise them in congressional testimony as "courageous leaders" in the War on Terror—approached the CIA with an extraordinary proposal: release Shakir and try to flip him. That is, allow him to return to Iraq on the condition that he agrees to report back on the activities of Iraqi intelligence.

It was a plan fraught with obvious risks. Shakir was a potentially valuable link between Saddam Hussein's regime and al Qaeda's September 11 plot. Even if he wasn't working for Iraqi intelligence, Shakir was one of a small group of terrorists still alive who might have had firsthand knowledge of the details of the Kuala Lumpur meeting. Could someone involved, however indirectly, in the worst terrorist attack in American history, and who was found with contact information for terrorists involved in several other attacks on America, be trusted to report back to Jordanian and U.S. intelligence officials on Iraqi intelligence?

In one of the most egregious mistakes by the U.S. intelligence community after September 11, the CIA agreed to release Shakir. He posted a modest bail and returned to Iraq.

Ahmed Hikmat Shakir hasn't been heard from since.

CHAPTER TWO

A SKEPTICAL PRESS

Imagine this scenario. The U.S. intelligence community receives a document scooped up from the Baghdad headquarters of the Mukhabarat—the Iraqi Intelligence Service—after the war in Iraq. It lists individuals from Kuwait and Saudi Arabia whom the Iraqi regime considers intelligence assets. The dossier includes Osama bin Laden. A leading U.S. intelligence agency determines that the document is authentic.

Such a find would be front-page news, right? Newspapers across the country would announce the discovery in dramatic headlines: "Partners in Terror: Documents Reveal Saddam-Osama Connection." The revelation would lead newscasts on each of the big three television networks. The cable news channels, always eager for breaking stories, might even interrupt a talk show. Pictures of Saddam and Osama would be splashed across the covers of *Time, U.S. News & World Report,* and *Newsweek.*

On March 28, 1992, the Mukhabarat compiled such a list. It is twenty pages long, with "Top Secret" marked at the top of each page. On page 14 is a now-familiar name: Osama bin Laden. The authors of the document assert that bin Laden "is in good relationship with our section in Syria." The list was recovered after the war by the Iraqi National Congress—a group long opposed to Saddam Hussein—and turned over to U.S. officials. The Defense Intelligence Agency has determined that the document is authentic.

The reaction to that document by the establishment media and the U.S. intelligence community provides a revealing look at the treatment of the broader Iraq–al Qaeda links.

The DIA dismissed the inclusion of bin Laden as "insignificant" because it didn't include any additional information on the relationship between him and Iraqi intelligence. Still, reporters who obtained copies of the document were cautioned against republishing it in full. Why? Because the FBI and DIA are investigating the scores of other people listed and their connections with Iraqi intelligence. How is it possible that bin Laden's inclusion on the list is "insignificant," but the other names are potentially so significant that two U.S. intelligence agencies are investigating their potential connections with Iraqi intelligence?

Eleven months after the list was put together, six people were killed and more than one thousand injured in a bombing at the World Trade Center. A top secret CIA document concludes that a "solid case" exists that al Qaeda operatives conducted the attacks. Fragmentary evidence points to Iraqi involvement. An Iraqi terrorist admitted mixing the chemicals for the bomb. Another conspirator made forty-six phone calls to Iraq two months before the plot's masterminds arrived in the United States—one of them from Baghdad. One of the bombers returned to Baghdad with the active assistance of the Iraqi embassy in Amman, Jordan, and received safe haven and financial support from the Iraqi regime for nearly a decade after those attacks.

It may be that this was a series of strange coincidences. But doesn't this set of facts, coupled with the new revelation that Iraq considered bin Laden an intelligence asset, merit further inquiry by the media and the intelligence community?

The document's first media mention came on March 7, 2004, on CBS News's *60 Minutes*. But the report was buried several minutes into a story about Ahmed Chalabi and his Iraqi National Congress and took up just thirty seconds in the ten-minute piece. News reporters might have followed up with a simple report on the existence of the document. Enterprising investigative journalists might have looked into why the Iraqi regime considered bin Laden an asset.

Instead, the story ended there. As of this writing, only the *Washington Times* has mentioned that the document exists.

Not all reporters ignored the Iraq–al Qaeda connection. Many instead seemed determined to discredit each claim made by the Bush administration even when those claims had the explicit support of the U.S. intelligence community.

The most important thing to know about media coverage of Iraq's links to al Qaeda is just how few reporters have followed the contours of this story closely. White House reporters and general assignment reporters in Washington have covered it occasionally—when President Bush cites the connection in a speech or a press briefing. Most of the reporting on Iraq–al Qaeda relations has fallen to a handful of reporters on the intelligence beats at major daily newspapers such as the *Washington Post* and the *New York Times*. The weekly news magazines, too, have occasionally reported on the connection.

Almost without exception, reporters at these agenda-setting publications have refused to be swayed by emerging evidence of the links, and in some cases, they are transparently dismissive. If the *New York Times* and the *Washington Post* report that the links are dubious, so do reporters and producers from the TV networks and writers from regional newspapers.

Of all the stories expressing skepticism of Iraq–al Qaeda connections, the most influential was the one that ran on the front page of the *New York Times* on June 9, 2003, under the headline "Captives Deny Qaeda Worked with Baghdad." Versions of the story ran in newspapers across the country, and cable networks touted the scoop on their running news tickers.

When the Carnegie Endowment for International Peace compiled a report on alleged prewar deceptions, the *Times* piece was exhibit A in support of its widely covered claim that the Bush administration hyped the Iraq–al Qaeda connection. The article may have been behind Al Gore's claim, in a speech at NYU two months after the piece was published, that "the evidence now shows clearly that Saddam did not want to work with Osama bin Laden at all, much less give him weapons of mass destruction."

For journalists and politicians long dubious of the connection, the *Times* story gave them additional reasons to be skeptical. But the article told half the story.

> Two of the highest-ranking leaders of al Qaeda in American custody have told the CIA in separate interrogations that the terrorist organization did not work jointly with the Iraqi government of Saddam Hussein, according to several intelligence officials.

Abu Zubaydah, a Qaeda planner and recruiter until his capture in March 2002, told his questioners last year that the idea of working with Mr. Hussein's government had been discussed among Qaeda leaders, but that Osama bin Laden had rejected such proposals, according to an official who has read the Central Intelligence Agency's classified report on the interrogation.

In his debriefing, Mr. Zubaydah said Mr. bin Laden had vetoed the idea because he did not want to be beholden to Mr. Hussein, the official said.

Separately, Khalid Sheikh Mohammed, the Qaeda chief of operations until his capture on March 1 in Pakistan, has also told interrogators that the group did not work with Mr. Hussein, officials said.

The Bush administration has not made these statements public, though it frequently highlighted intelligence reports that supported its assertions of links between Iraq and Al Qaeda as it made its case for war against Iraq.

Some of the most misleading coverage of the Iraq–al Qaeda connection involves the debriefings of high-level detainees. All the information obtained in such debriefings should, of course, be received with great skepticism. Ideally, interrogators extract information from a detainee and test it against a set of facts, often information obtained from other detainees. Detainees are then determined to be credible, partly credible, or not credible. The information they provide is judged accordingly.

Most journalists are not privy to those assessments. There is thus an inclination to give credence to reports from detainees that confirm the reporter's own prejudices and to ignore or downplay reports that contradict them.

The *Times* story also underscores the erroneous assumption the intelligence officials are disinterested actors whose assessments are somehow above politics.

Abu Zubaydah, one of the detainees cited in the *Times* piece, did indeed tell U.S. interrogators that bin Laden had misgivings about working with Saddam. But he also provided a host of hollow warnings and other reports that investigators later concluded were false and designed to cause panic. Even if Zubaydah was not flatly lying about the relationship between Iraq and al Qaeda, his statements were far more nuanced than the *Times* story indicated. Zubaydah told his interrogators that bin Laden had rejected the idea of a "formal alliance" with Saddam. But the absence of such an arrangement hardly precludes cooperation. And the next sentence of the classified summary of the debriefing changes its meaning significantly.

"This said, bin Laden views any entity which hated Americans or was willing to kill them as an ally," the report said. Further, Abu Zubaydah explained that bin Laden's "personal goal of destroying the U.S. is so strong that to achieve this end he would work with whomever could help him, so long as al Qaeda's independence was not threatened."

The CIA report later adds that Zubaydah "admitted that it was entirely possible that there were communications or emissaries" of which he would not be aware. Most striking, Zubaydah confirmed that bin Laden "approved of contacts and funding" for Jund al Islam, a militant Islamic group in northern Iraq that battled the two anti-Saddam Kurdish factions. Jund al Islam, later known as Ansar al Islam, received money and arms from the former Iraqi regime. The third-ranking official in the group, a man known as Abu Wael, was also an officer in the Iraqi Intelligence Service.

So Abu Zubaydah's debriefing was at least a mixed bag. And some of the information he provided, when tested against other reporting, strongly suggests that Iraq and al Qaeda were working together.

Readers of the *Times* that day came away with the opposite impression. How? The story suggested that the Bush administration selectively presented intelligence to make its case about Iraq–al Qaeda collaboration. That *Times* sources apparently presented the reporter with only half of the debriefing suggests that they were guilty of precisely the same offense.

If the *Times* story helped establish a new national mind-set on Iraq–al Qaeda connections, the conventional wisdom solidified with the extraordinary coverage of an appearance by Vice President Dick Cheney on NBC's *Meet the Press* on September 14, 2003.

With three words—"We don't know"—Cheney set off a media firestorm. He was responding to a question from host Tim Russert.

RUSSERT: The *Washington Post* asked the American people about Saddam Hussein, and this is what they said:

69 percent said he was involved in the September 11 attacks. Are you surprised by that?

CHENEY: No. I think it's not surprising that people make
that connection.

RUSSERT: But is there a connection?

CHENEY: We don't know. You and I talked about this two
years ago. I can remember you asking me this question
just a few days after the original attack. At the time I
said no, we didn't have any evidence of that. Subsequent
to that, we've learned a couple of things. We learned
more and more that there was a relationship between
Iraq and al Qaeda that stretched back through most of
the decade of the '90s, that it involved training, for example, on BW [biological weapons] and CW [chemical
weapons], that al Qaeda sent personnel to Baghdad to
get trained on the systems that are involved, the Iraqis
providing bomb-making expertise and advice to the
al Qaeda organization . . . With respect to 9/11, of
course, we've had the story that's been public out there.
The Czechs alleged that Mohamed Atta, the lead at-
tacker, met in Prague with a senior Iraqi intelligence official five months before the attack, but we've never
been able to develop any more of that yet either in terms
of confirming it or discrediting it. We just don't know.

To many viewers that day, Cheney's answer must have
seemed straightforward, even refreshing. It's not every day that
a politician—let alone the vice president—admits on national
television that the government is dealing with imperfect or in-

complete knowledge on one of the key issues of the time. Although this should come as no surprise, the reality is that many decisions are made without the benefit of perfect knowledge. This is especially true of decisions made on the basis of intelligence.

Journalists didn't see it that way. The next day, the *Washington Post* dissected Cheney's performance in a front-page article that was ostensibly straight news, but read like a press release from the Democratic National Committee. The story, written by Dana Milbank and Walter Pincus, the paper's most tenacious Bush administration critics, amounted to a nearly point-by-point repudiation of Cheney's arguments. It accused Cheney of dishonestly resurrecting questionable arguments to justify the war in Iraq. The reporters concluded that Cheney seemed "to broaden the intelligence on other alleged al Qaeda connections with Hussein," when he claimed that "the Iraqi government and the Iraqi intelligence service had a relationship with al Qaeda that stretched back through most of the decade of the '90s."

If the *Post* reporters merely hinted at Cheney's alleged mendacity, other journalists were less restrained. In the weeks after the show, Cheney was accused of lying, inventing facts, disregarding intelligence, and reviving discredited conspiracy theories. And that was just in the straight, ostensibly "objective" news stories.

Cheney's appearance on *Meet the Press* is a good case study of exaggeration, hyperbole, and even outright duplicity. But not in the way that most journalists imagined. There was plenty of overstatement and hype, but it came not from Cheney, but from many of the reporters and pundits covering his appearance.

Reporters quoted Cheney out of context and mischaracterized his meaning. Headline writers had him making allegations that never passed his lips. Columnists put words in Cheney's mouth and then suggested he lied.

Two days after the appearance on *Meet the Press* and one day after the *Post* article, the *Boston Globe* ran an article on its front page under the headline, "Cheney Link of Iraq, 9/11 Challenged." It was a sexy headline and one that might help sell newspapers. But it also overstated Cheney's claims, as even the first sentence of the article makes clear.

"Vice President Dick Cheney, anxious to defend the White House foreign policy amid ongoing violence in Iraq, stunned intelligence analysts and even members of his own administration this week by failing to dismiss a widely discredited claim: that Saddam Hussein might have played a role in the Sept. 11 attacks."

Positively making a "link" between Iraq and September 11, as the headline suggests, is hardly the same as "failing to dismiss" the possibility that such a link exists. But that nuance was largely lost on the *Globe* reporters, who seemed to doubt that Iraq had any connection at all to al Qaeda. "Details that Cheney cited to make the case that the Iraqi dictator had ties to Al Qaeda have been dismissed by the CIA as having no basis, according to analysts and officials," they wrote.

It wasn't just the news pages that distorted Cheney's comments. At least the *Los Angeles Times* saved its editorializing for the editorial page. "Vice President Dick Cheney . . . upheld sweeping, unproven claims about Saddam Hussein's connections to terrorism." Cheney, the paper went on, "seems stuck in a time warp." His claim that Iraq and al Qaeda had been in league for much of the 1990s was dubious, the writers claimed, because it represented "a more sweeping time frame than others in the administration have ventured."

On September 17, 2003, Joshua Micah Marshall, an insightful left-leaning opinion columnist for *The Hill* newspaper, seemed to articulate what these reporters and opinion writers somehow felt too constrained to state baldly. "By any reasonable standard, that's a lie," he wrote of Cheney's claim that "we don't know" about potential Iraqi involvement in the September 11 attacks. "American intelligence and law enforcement have been investigating the Sept. 11 attacks for more than two years and we haven't found a single shred of evidence tying Saddam or his regime to the plot. Nothing."

Was Cheney misleading the American public on national television? Many of the nation's top political reporters and editorialists clearly believed he was. It didn't take long for academics to join in.

Paul Waldman, author of several books on the press and public opinion, suggested the Bush administration might be guilty of something called "enthymematic argumentation." In a *Washington Post* opinion piece on September 28, 2003, Waldman argued, "in an enthymeme, the speaker builds an argument with one element removed, leading listeners to fill in the missing piece." Each time the Bush administration coupled Iraq and September 11, this theory goes, the American people made the direct connection on their own. "We were attacked on Sept. 11, so we went to war against Iraq. The missing piece of the argument—'Saddam was involved in 9/11'—didn't have to be said aloud for those listening to assimilate its message."

It's a very interesting theory, to be sure. It's also very silly.

Most Americans viewed national security threats differently after the September 11 attacks. This was true not only of Dick Cheney and other Republicans, but of many Democrats, too. Democratic politicians rhetorically linked September 11 and the war in Iraq dozens of times—not because they were participating in a clever Bush administration plot to deceive the country, but because those attacks, as so many Americans have put it, "changed everything." Hillary Clinton made the connection in the Senate floor speech she gave upon voting for the Iraq War. Noting that New Yorkers are acutely aware of the dangers of terror, she said Saddam Hussein has given "aid, comfort and sanctuary to terrorists, including al Qaeda members."

Even the French made the connection. "You must not underestimate the shockwave that was September 11 and the feeling of insecurity Americans have everywhere in the world," said French foreign minister Dominique de Villepin, on French radio on November 12, 2002, shortly after his country voted to approve a UN resolution giving Iraq one last chance to disarm. "The security of America is under threat from people like Saddam Hussein who are capable of using chemical and biological weapons."

Contrary to the allegations leveled in the press, the vice president said very little that other top officials in the administration and in the intelligence community hadn't said before. Both CIA director George Tenet and secretary of state Colin Powell agreed with Cheney that the relationship dated back to the early 1990s. Tenet, in a letter to the Senate Intelligence Committee on October 7, 2002, reported that the intelligence community had accumulated "solid reporting of senior-level contacts between Iraq and al Qaeda going back a decade."

Powell spoke of "decades-long experience with respect to ties between Iraq and al Qaeda," in his February 5, 2003, presentation at the UN Security Council. "Going back to the early and mid-1990s when bin Laden was based in Sudan, an al Qaeda source tells us that Saddam and bin Laden reached an understanding that al Qaeda would no longer support activities against Baghdad. Early al Qaeda ties were forged by secret high-level intelligence service contacts with al Qaeda."

More important, neither Powell nor Tenet, in their public statements, would rule out the possibility of Iraqi complicity in the September 11 attacks. "There is no doubt that there has been contacts and linkages to the al Qaeda organization," Tenet told the Senate Armed Services Committee on March 19, 2002. "As to where we are on September 11, the jury's still out. And, as I said carefully in my statement, it would be a mistake to dismiss the possibility of state sponsorship, whether Iranian, or Iraqi[,] and we'll see where the evidence takes us."

Powell addressed the question of possible Iraqi involvement in the September 11 attacks at a hearing of the Senate Foreign Relations Committee six months later, on September 26, 2002. Several senators had raised questions about the credibility of the administration's case connecting Iraq to al Qaeda. Powell, speaking cautiously about the allegations, left open the possibility of Iraqi involvement. "There is evidence of linkage between al Qaeda and Iraq," Powell told the panel. He added: "There is no linkage to 9/11 that we are aware of, but I can't dismiss that possibility." He reiterated the point moments later. "There's no smoking-gun linkage to 9/11, but it cannot totally be ruled out."

None of this mattered to the media, which had by the time Cheney appeared on *Meet the Press* settled on a simple story line about the Iraq–al Qaeda connection: the Bush administration, led by Cheney and a cabal of "neoconservatives," exaggerated the relationship to frighten an unwitting nation into supporting a war in Iraq.

The trumped-up controversy showed no signs of dying its own death when President Bush was asked about Cheney's comments three days after the vice president's *Meet the Press* appearance.

"We've had no evidence that Saddam Hussein was involved with September the eleventh," Bush said prior to a cabinet meeting on September 17, 2003. "Now, what the vice president said was—is that [Saddam] has been involved with al Qaeda and [Abu Musab] al-Zarqawi, an al Qaeda operative[,] was in Baghdad. He's the guy that ordered the killing of a U.S. diplomat. He's a man who's still running loose involved with the poisons network, involved with Ansar al-Islam. There's no question that Saddam Hussein had al Qaeda ties."

Bush's comments dominated the day's news coverage. On *NBC Nightly News*, anchor Tom Brokaw told millions of Americans that Bush admitted "there is no connection between Saddam Hussein and the attacks of 9/11." But Bush, of course, said no such thing. What the president did say was the U.S. government "had no evidence" of an Iraqi connection. It may seem like a small difference, but it is not. Not having evidence is quite different from saying such evidence does not exist.

Dan Bartlett, the White House communications director, and Scott McClellan, the White House press secretary, would later say privately that they should have advised the president to acknowledge only a lack of "proof." There is, in fact, evidence of Iraqi involvement in the September 11 attacks, though it is circumstantial and highly speculative.

The damage was already done. The president's comment was widely reported as a rebuke to Cheney. Helen Thomas, the veteran White House correspondent and columnist for Hearst Newspapers, wrote, "Poof! In an instant the president knocked the stuffing from one of his stated reasons for leading the United States to war against Iraq."

And the *New York Times,* like many other media outlets, reported that Bush had tried to "correct" Cheney's statement. But unlike other reporters, *Times* writer David E. Sanger put the issue in proper perspective. "The White House has never said Mr. Hussein was part of the Sept. 11 plot, though from the moment of the attacks there was a search to determine whether he was linked."

Not only had the Bush administration carefully avoided claiming that Hussein was involved in the September 11 attacks, the president's assertion wasn't even new. Reporters from *Newsweek* magazine put the question to Bush directly on January 31, 2003, two months *before* the war and nine months prior to the feeding frenzy after Cheney's *Meet the Press* appearance. "I cannot make that claim," was Bush's direct response.

The story refused to die. Attempts to keep it alive ranged from the desperate to the bizarre. On September 29, 2003, two weeks after Cheney's *Meet the Press* appearance, *Washington Post* reporters Dana Priest and Glenn Kessler wrote a long, front-page news article focusing on his comments. The headline? "Iraq, 9/11 Still Linked by Cheney."

The reporters critically examined Cheney's arguments about Iraq's links to al Qaeda and, more specifically, his allusions to the alleged meeting between Mohamed Atta and an Iraqi intelligence agent in Prague. Many in the media have long been skeptical of such a meeting, and their coverage frequently exposes this bias. The Czechs, Kessler and Priest reported, had privately expressed doubts about their initial reporting on the encounter.

"The vice president's role in keeping the alleged meeting in Prague before the public eye is an illustration of the administration's handling of intelligence reports in the run-up to the war," they argued, "when senior officials sometimes seized on reports that bolstered the case against Iraq despite contradictory evidence provided by the U.S. intelligence community."

To back up this claim, the *Post* reporters contrasted Cheney's comments about the Prague meeting to those made in a speech delivered by FBI director Robert S. Mueller III.

"[Mueller] told a San Francisco audience, 'We ran down literally hundreds of thousands of leads and checked every record we could get our hands on, from flight reservations to car rentals to bank accounts.' The FBI, he said, could find no evidence that Atta left or returned to the United States at the time."

Their point was clear: Cheney dismissed assessments like Mueller's when they conflicted with his political arguments.

One problem. Mueller never commented on Atta's alleged trip to Prague in the speech cited by the *Post*. The speech, delivered to the Commonwealth Club on April 19, 2002, contained no reference whatsoever to the alleged meeting. Mueller referred to Afghanistan and Germany, the Philippines, Paris, and Pakistan. But he never mentioned the Czech Republic or Prague. And he never mentioned Iraq. In fact, Mueller never even mentioned Atta by name. Here is the relevant passage:

> We realized that we had to conduct this investigation somewhat differently. These attacks were not just an act of terror. They were an act of war. The most pressing issue for the FBI and for the nation was to find out who we were at war with, and more importantly, to make sure we were not attacked again.
>
> To do that, the FBI began working in concert with its many partners to find out everything we could about the hijackers and how they pulled off their attacks. We ran down literally hundreds of thousands of leads and checked every record we could get our hands on, from flight reservations to car rentals to bank accounts.
>
> What emerged from our massive investigation was a sobering portrait of 19 hijackers who carried out their attacks with meticulous planning, extraordinary secrecy, and extensive knowledge of how America works.

Neither Mueller nor CIA director George Tenet has ever ruled out the Prague meeting. Indeed, Tenet has repeatedly gone to great lengths to emphasize that the intelligence on the alleged meeting is vague and inconclusive. Cheney, in his *Meet the Press* interview, made this clear. "We've never been able to develop any more of that either in terms of confirming it or discrediting it."

Priest returned to the theme of Cheney as a serial exaggerator in an article on January 14, 2004. "Vice President Cheney has sought to publicly link Hussein with al Qaeda and has repeatedly suggested that Iraq somehow participated in the September 11, 2001, terrorist attacks against the United States," she alleged. "This view is disputed in intelligence reports, which state that there is no evidence linking Iraq to the attacks on the World Trade Center and the Pentagon or to al Qaeda's worldwide operations."

There are, contrary to Priest's assertion, literally hundreds of intelligence reports detailing links between Iraq and al Qaeda's worldwide operations. There are numerous others that present evidence—again, much of it circumstantial and speculative—about potential Iraqi involvement in September 11.

Despite these reports, Cheney has never claimed that Iraq "somehow participated" in the September 11 attacks. Indeed, in almost every interview he has given on the subject of September 11 and Iraq's ties to al Qaeda, Cheney has carefully separated the two issues. This was true in the days immediately following the September 11 attacks and it was true as late as January 9, 2004, five days *before* the Priest article when Cheney gave an interview to M. E. Sprengelmeyer of the *Rocky Mountain News*. The vice president was asked directly about Iraq, al Qaeda, and 9/11:

Well, there are two issues here . . . in terms of relationship. One is, was there a relationship between al Qaeda and Iraq, between Osama bin Laden and Saddam Hussein, or the al Qaeda and the Iraqi intelligence service? That's one category of issues. A separate question is, whether or not there was any relationship relative to 9/11. Those are two separate questions and people oftentimes confuse them.

On the separate issue, on the 9/11 question, we've never had confirmation one way or another. We did have reporting that was public, that came out shortly after the 9/11 attack, provided by the Czech government, suggesting there had been a meeting in Prague between Mohamed Atta, the lead hijacker, and a man named al-Ani [Ahmed Khalil Ibrahim Samir al Ani], who was an Iraqi intelligence official in Prague, at the embassy there, in April of '01, prior to the 9/11 attacks. It has never been—we've never been able to collect any more information on that. That was the one that possibly tied the two together to 9/11.

Priest still wasn't convinced. During a March 10, 2004, appearance on MSNBC's *Hardball*, host Chris Matthews asked her about Cheney's comments to the *Rocky Mountain News*. Priest responded, "Well, you have picked out some of the more tangential issues like the *Rocky Mountain News*. What about all of those national broadcasts that the vice president went on and suggested that there was a definite link between 9/11 and Iraq and al Qaeda and Iraq?"

Priest didn't name "all of those national broadcasts." That is not surprising since, as noted, Cheney has never suggested that there was a "definite link between 9/11 and Iraq."

Many journalists also accepted uncritically the comfortable notion that because of their significant differences over religion, Saddam Hussein and Osama bin Laden would not cooperate. But in testimony before the Senate Armed Services Committee given on February 12, 2003, CIA director George

Tenet disagreed: "It's a distinction that people have tried to make, particularly in the terrorism world, which I don't think very much of."

In the days leading up to the war in Iraq, NPR's Tom Gjelten spoke with "intelligence officials" who "say that Saddam's intelligence service had contacts with many nefarious groups, in part, to keep track of them. Al Qaeda is a radical Islamist group. Saddam had a secular regime; he may have felt threatened by them, and it would have been quite logical for him to want to sort of keep tabs on these groups, in part, by having contacts with them."

Daniel Benjamin and Steven Simon, authors of *The Age of Sacred Terror*, weighed in with an op-ed piece in the *New York Times*. "As members of the National Security Council staff from 1994 to 1999, we closely examined nearly a decade's worth of intelligence and we became convinced, like many of our colleagues in the intelligence community, that the religious radicals of al Qaeda and the secularists of Baathist Iraq simply did not trust one another or share sufficiently compelling interests to work together."

Why did the media get Cheney's *Meet the Press* appearance so wrong? And what accounts for the unbridled media cynicism on Iraq's links to al Qaeda? They are separate but related questions.

By the time Cheney appeared on *Meet the Press*, American troops had been in control of Iraq for five months and had not yet found the stockpiles of Saddam's weapons of mass destruction the administration had promised before the war. Journalists felt betrayed and used. With only a few exceptions, reporters had generally shared the assumption that WMD would be found in vast quantities after Saddam was deposed. That's not surprising. The entire world thought Saddam possessed WMD. Among those who articulated this belief were former president Bill Clinton, UN inspectors, French foreign minister Dominique de Villepin, and Senator John Kerry. The CIA, along with nearly every other intelligence agency in the world, agreed. "I think we will find caches of weapons of mass destruction," said CIA director George Tenet, in congressional testimony one month before the war. "Absolutely."

On February 11, 2004, a year to the day after Tenet's testimony, Jami Miscik, the deputy director of intelligence at the CIA, offered a candid internal assessment of the failure to find WMD in a speech to analysts. "The single most important aspect of our tradecraft that needs to be examined," she said, is a reliance on "inherited assumptions." "How do we ensure that we are not passing along assumptions that haven't been sufficiently questioned or reexamined?"

Miscik didn't address Iraq–al Qaeda links, but the malady she identifies—a dependence on "inherited assumptions"—also explains why the CIA consistently underreported the relationship. For years, CIA bureaucrats had assumed that Saddam and bin Laden, divided by differences in religious ideology, would never work together. But journalists felt burned and eventually settled on one story line: Bush administration officials misled us, often deliberately, to persuade the nation to support its determination to go to war in Iraq. The Bush administration contributed to this perception by failing to deal in a straightforward manner with questions about a line in President Bush's 2003 State of the Union Address: "The

British government has learned that Saddam Hussein recently sought significant quantities of uranium from Africa."

The statement, while technically true, had been the subject of interagency squabbling before the speech because intelligence analysts had differing views about the credibility and significance of the report. What's more, another report about Saddam's alleged attempts to procure uranium from Niger had been based on a forgery.

When the Bush administration faced questions about the claim, top officials offered a wide variety of explanations and justifications. The usually disciplined Bush White House was not "on message," and they paid for it.

Journalists took this incident and reasoned from it that many of the other rationales for the war were fraudulent. In an analysis breathtaking in its candor, *The Note,* a widely read on-line publication put out by ABC News, summarized the media coverage in its February 10, 2004, issue. "The press, by and large, does not accept President Bush's justifications for the Iraq war—in any of its WMD, imminent threat, or evil-doer formulations."

CHAPTER THREE

SADDAM FINDS RELIGION

It is true that Saddam Hussein and Osama bin Laden were strange bedfellows. Bin Laden, after all, labeled Hussein an "infidel" on several occasions. Hussein imprisoned and executed thousands of Islamic clerics over his thirty-year reign of terror.

But it's one thing to acknowledge that bin Laden and Hussein were not natural allies; it's quite another to conclude that the two would therefore never work together. Yet that has been the erroneous assumption behind the CIA assessments of the relationship for more than a decade. Journalists, with a few notable exceptions, have worked from the same flawed premise. If nothing else, the active collaboration of al Qaeda operatives and secular Baathists in postwar Iraq would seem to disprove that thesis.

A brief look at the history of Saddam's rule in Iraq demonstrates that he was not above using Islam and the language and practices of the mujahideen when it suited his purposes. He actively supported Syrian religious extremists in their efforts to overthrow Syrian despot Hafez al Assad, a longtime rival who had backed Iran in the Iran-Iraq War. In 1982, Assad brutally put down a rebellion in Hama led by the Syrian Muslim Brotherhood, a radical Islamic group opposed to his secular regime. Estimates of the death toll range from five thousand to twenty-five thousand. The group dispersed, with its more moderate elements relocating to Jordan, Saudi Arabia, and a number of European countries. The radicals, including several of the group's leaders, moved to Iraq, where they were welcomed by Saddam Hussein. Syrian Muslim Brothers trained with Iraqis at the al Rashdiya camp outside Baghdad.

According to U.S. officials and press reports, one of the Syrians who spent time at the Iraqi camp is Imad Eddin Barakat Yarkas. Yarkas, captured in Madrid in November 2001, was the leader of al Qaeda's operations in Spain. The roommate of lead hijacker Mohamed Atta in Germany, he was believed by Spanish and American authorities to have been directly involved in planning and financing the September 11 attacks. Indeed, many leaders of the al Qaeda cells in Madrid and Hamburg, Germany—the cells that executed the September 11 attacks—are onetime Syrian Muslim Brothers.

There is no indication that Yarkas stayed in close contact with the Iraqi regime after he left in 1986. But some of the leadership of the Syrian Muslim Brotherhood did. On May 5, 1998, Iraqi state-run television reported that vice president Taha Yasin Ramadan met with leaders of the Brotherhood in Baghdad. And as late as February 2000, the Syrian Muslim Brotherhood's leaders spoke openly about their presence in Iraq.

(In a side note, when Spanish authorities seized documents from top al Qaeda operatives in Spain in November 2001, they found an invitation to a party at the residence of the Iraqi ambassador to Spain. The invitation went to Luis Galan Gonzalez, a Spanish convert to Islam who worked for Yarkas, under Gonzalez's al Qaeda nom de guerre, Yusuf Galan.)

Saddam's provision of safe haven to the group is insignificant on an operational level, as the Syrian Muslim Brotherhood is not believed to have conducted any significant attacks for years. But his tolerance of their presence in Iraq is one of many indications that he was not as hostile to Islamic radicals as conventional wisdom suggests. Throughout Iraq's war with Iran, from 1980 to 1988, the Iranian clerics sought to present Saddam not only as an aggressor, but as an infidel whose words and actions were anticlerical and anti-Islam. To counter this criticism, Saddam made some modest adjustments to his rhetoric, inserting religious praise and otherwise invoking Allah as he battled his neighbors.

Saddam further Islamized his image and his regime in the run-up to Iraq's invasion of Kuwait and the subsequent Gulf War. At least rhetorically, Saddam went from an outspoken secularist to a fiery jihadist.

Amatzia Baram, currently a scholar at the U.S. Institute for Peace, is perhaps the world's greatest authority on Saddam Hussein. He has detailed Saddam's transformation in dozens of articles and books, including an analysis published in the December 2000 issue of the *Middle East Review of International Affairs.*

President Saddam Husayn led the Ba'th party in introducing some Islamic principles into the Iraqi legal system. This started a short while before the invasion of Kuwait in 1990, when Saddam made clear that whenever laws clashed with the divine Shari'a [Islamic law], the former must always give way. One day before the Allied bombing began the fighting in January 1991, Saddam Husayn added the slogan, "Allahu Akbar" (God is Great) to the Iraqi national flag. During the war, Saddam's rhetoric was fully Islamized in a way unparalleled by any other Arab secular leader.

Baram notes that Saddam undertook a wide-ranging public relations campaign to cast himself as an Islamic holy warrior. He frequently invoked past Islamic battles and rallied Muslims to his cause by claiming that he would return the Islamic world to glory by taking the battle to the Western infidels.

Following the Iraqi defeat in the war, there was no sign of a return to rational, secular rhetoric. Indeed, in 1994, when the economic embargo resulted in serious inflating and unprecedented suffering among the vast majority of Iraqis, Saddam Husayn went further by introducing punishments such as severing the right hand for theft and the death penalty for prostitution, defining these penalties as Islamic. The Iraqi president also initiated laws forbidding the public consumption of alcohol and introduced enhanced compulsory study of the Qur'an at all educational levels, including in Ba'th party branches . . . It is impossible to gauge the extent to which the "Islamization" steps helped the Iraqi president and his ruling elite stay in power by more effectively legitimizing them. It would seem, however, that such a far-reaching decision had to be based on a rational calculation that more emphasis on Islam would strengthen the regime's popularity.

Hussein Kamel, Saddam's son-in-law, complained of these efforts when he defected in August 1995. "The government of Iraq is instigating fundamentalism in the country," he told Rolf Ekeus, then head of the UN weapons inspection program. "It is against Europe and U.S. Now, Baath Party members have to pass a religious exam. This would strengthen Iran. It would be detrimental to the whole region. This will be another world war. Every party member has to pass a religious exam. They even stopped party meetings for prayers."

Saddam did more than tweak his rhetoric and change some laws to court Islamic radicals. "Saddam did make a serious attempt to make in-roads with the extremists," says Dr. Stanley Bedlington, who served as a senior analyst and chief of foreign liaison at the CIA's counterterrorism center from 1986 to 1994. Bedlington neither dismisses nor affirms the notion that Saddam and al Qaeda had a working relationship. "I have an open mind about it," he says. "They were not ideologically compatible. On the other hand, we do know that al Qaeda operatives had been placed in Baghdad. Their hatred of the United States alone could bring them to work together."

Beginning in June 1990, Saddam inaugurated a series of "Popular Islamic Conferences" in Baghdad. In many respects, the summits were like professional association meetings in the West. But instead of discussing "best practices" of hardware sales or Kiwanis Club community service projects, the Baghdad breakouts focused on terror. Some of the attendees were simply low-level bureaucrats in religious ministries from the region. But others were proud terrorists, from a wide variety of murderous Islamist groups, who openly called for a jihad against the United States. The conferences were called, sometimes hastily, when Saddam needed to demonstrate his support among terrorists. The intended message was not subtle: mess with me and you mess with them.

One such conference ended on January 13, 1991, four days before the Gulf War. With hundreds of thousands of American soldiers on Iraq's borders, the clerics ended the conference with a call for "holy war" should the coalition attack. Six days later, the general secretariat of the conference issued a statement calling jihad the duty of all Muslims. Baghdad radio echoed this appeal, calling on Muslims to strike "interests, facilities, symbols and figures" of the coalition countries. It worked.

"Hurry, and strike at and destroy the interests of U.S. imperialists and their allies," said Abu Abbas, leader of the Palestinian Liberation Front, on January 19, 1991. (Abbas, who masterminded the hijacking of the *Achille Lauro* cruise ship in 1985, had been given safe haven by Saddam's regime and was captured in Baghdad by U.S. forces in April 2003.)

"Saddam enjoys wide support among fundamentalists in the Arab world who perceive the Western presence in the region as a threat to their society and culture," Salah Nasrawi, a reporter with the Associated Press, wrote that same day. Senator David L. Boren, a Democrat from Oklahoma who was then chairman of the Senate Intelligence Committee, spoke to the *Washington Post* about the collaboration on January 19, 1991, after receiving a two-hour briefing from senior intelligence officials.

"Saddam has put in place a network involving some of the most sophisticated terrorist organizations in the world," he said, adding that the effort was "pretty highly controlled, pretty highly disciplined."

"I don't think we're dealing with a terrorist army, but a small group of highly trained people who can do a lot of damage," said Paul Wilkerson, a noted terrorism expert, in the same *Washington Post* article. "Saddam has been building links with terrorist organizations for many months, so the possibility of giving them the backup of Iraqi secret services and diplomatic assets is quite real."

Even as Saddam was enlisting Islamic radicals in his cause, his own intelligence service began carrying out attacks. On January 18, 1991, the day after the Gulf War began, police in Indonesia defused a bomb planted in a flower box below a window of the U.S. ambassador's residence in Jakarta. An Iraqi operative had secretly inserted himself into a team of laborers renovating the home and buried twenty-six sticks of TNT in the dirt. (Meanwhile, Ambassador John Monjo "sat in his bay window drinking a stinger—whiskey and soda," recalls the CIA's Bedlington.) "He didn't bury it completely," says Bedlington, "and the gardener found it before it was detonated." Reports cited a dead battery on the bomb's timer as the reason the attempt failed.

The following day, on January 19, 1991, Ahmed J. Ahmed and Abdul Kadham Saad, two Iraqi students living in the Philippines, attempted to detonate a bomb at a U.S. government building that housed the U.S. Information Service and the Thomas Jefferson Cultural Center in Manila. Muwufak al Ani, officially the consul general at the Iraqi embassy in Manila but unofficially a top intelligence operative in South Asia, met with the bombers at least five times in the days leading up to the planned attack. His car was used to deliver the bombers to within a few blocks of their target.

At about 6:30 P.M., the attackers strolled up Buenida Avenue in the heart of Manila's business district. One block short of the American facility, the duo stopped to check the bomb. Then, boom.

"They stopped and tinkered with the device, placed in a paper bag," explained Philippine police lieutenant Jack Nayra. "The bomb apparently exploded prematurely."

Ahmed blew himself up in the botched attack, which came to be known at the CIA as "Operation Dogmeat." Saad had been badly burned in the explosion and was taken to the emergency room at a Manila hospital. When the hospital staff asked Saad, who was carrying two sets of identification, whom they should notify about his condition, he directed them to the Iraqi embassy and recited the embassy's telephone number.

"They set the timer for minutes rather than hours," explains Bedlington, the former CIA senior counterterrorism analyst. "Part of [Ahmed's] body was spread all over a tree." The rest of it was found, an hour after the attack, on top of a nearby home. Police found an Iraqi passport of "Ahmed J. Ahmed, businessman" at the scene.

Two other Iraqis, Hisham Abdul Sattar and his brother, Husam, were later ordered out of the country on suspicions that they were involved in the planning of the attack. The brothers were sons of the former Iraqi ambassador to the Philippines, who was then posted in Somalia. The Philippine government also expelled Muwufak al Ani, the Iraqi consul general, saying it had "strong evidence" linking him to the attacks. Al Ani denied any involvement in the bombing, but his business card was found in the pocket of one of the bombers. Shortly before boarding a Malaysian Airlines flight to Kuala Lumpur, al Ani declared, "I finished my diplomacy and I will go fight." Al Ani then shouted: "Long live Saddam Hussein!"

Back in Baghdad the next day, Saddam stepped up his jihadist rhetoric. "It remains for us to tell all Arabs, all militant believers . . . wherever they may be that it is your duty to embark on holy war. . . . You should target their interests wherever they may be."

At a rally in Jordan on January 26, 1991, Nader Tamini, son of the founder of Islamic Jihad, called for martyrs. "Anyone who wants to enlist to go on a suicide mission against Western interests, especially in Europe, can now contact the Islamic Jihad movement," he told a group of one thousand Palestinians protesting the Gulf War.

Other small terrorist attacks against American targets took place throughout the world. They were carried out by the Iraqi Intelligence Service, radical fundamentalists, and, in some cases, both operating together. In Uganda, a bomb was tossed over a high wall onto a tennis court vacated moments earlier by U.S. ambassador John Burroughs. American and British banks were also the targets of numerous attacks. The Italian embassy in Lebanon was struck by a rocket-propelled grenade.

Bedlington says other attacks were foiled because Iraqi intelligence agents were too incompetent to pull them off. As part of the worldwide effort to attack American interests, Saddam assigned dozens of Iraqi intelligence operatives to two-man teams. Each Iraqi intelligence agent was paired with a member of the Baghdad-supported Arab Liberation Front (ALF) and sent traveling.

"The Iraqis had given them all passports," Bedlington explains, "but they were all in numerical sequence." Passport officials in countries friendly to the United States were put on notice, and the would-be terrorists, easily identified by their passport numbers, were rounded up two by two.

Saddam's support for terrorists of all stripes was so widely known that it became an issue in the 1992 presidential campaign. In a scathing speech one month before the election, Senator Al Gore, the Democrats' vice presidential candidate, accused the first Bush administration of "a blatant disregard for brutal terrorism" and "a dangerous blindness to the murderous ambitions of a despot." In all, Gore made more than a dozen specific references to Iraq-sponsored terrorism. He cited a study by the RAND Corporation that reported "an estimated 1,400 terrorists were operating openly out of Iraq."

Republican administrations over the past decade had propped up Saddam Hussein in his war against Iran, ignoring bountiful evidence of Hussein's horrors, Gore argued. Saddam Hussein, he exclaimed, "had already launched poison gas attacks repeatedly, and Bush looked the other way. He had already conducted extensive terrorism activities, and Bush had looked the other way. He was already deeply involved in the effort to acquire nuclear weapons and other weapons of mass destruction, and Bush knew it, but he looked the other way. Well, in my view, the Bush administration was acting in a manner directly opposite to what you would expect with all of the evidence that it had available to it at the time. Saddam Hussein's nature and intentions were perfectly visible."

Gore's critique didn't end with that speech. Over the final month of the campaign, he would insert snatches of that text into his stump speech, highlighting his opponents' complicity in building up Saddam. "President Bush had ample information early on to suggest that Saddam Hussein was a major danger to the region and to U.S. interests," Gore claimed in a speech on October 15, 1992, "including information that he was aggressively seeking technologies for weapons of mass destruction and that he was offering state payments to terrorists."

While much of Saddam's record of terrorist sponsorship was a matter of public record, many of his dealings were not. It was nearly a decade later that the world learned that Saddam invited Ayman al Zawahiri, "the Doctor," to Baghdad in 1992. At the time of his trip to Baghdad, Zawahiri, an Egyptian physician, was running Egyptian Islamic Jihad, an extremist group that merged with al Qaeda in 1998. Now Osama bin Laden's top deputy, he is the man many terrorism experts credit with making al Qaeda the lethal organization it became in the late 1990s.

The first detailed report of Zawahiri's trip came in a March 25, 2002, article in *The New Yorker* written by veteran reporter Jeffrey Goldberg. Goldberg traveled to Kurdish-controlled northern Iraq in early 2002 to report on Saddam's use of chemical weapons on Iraqi Kurds in Halabja at the end of the

Iran-Iraq War. In the course of his reporting, Goldberg would learn about a far more immediate threat. He was invited by one of the two rival Kurdish political parties, the Patriotic Union of Kurdistan, to interview prisoners who claimed detailed knowledge of collaboration, after the September 11 attacks, between Iraqi intelligence and al Qaeda.

One such prisoner was Qassem Hussein Muhammed, a twenty-year veteran of Iraqi intelligence. Qassem told Goldberg that he had been one of seventeen bodyguards assigned to protect Zawahiri on his 1992 trip. Zawahiri, according to Qassem, stayed at the al Rashid Hotel and traveled secretly throughout Baghdad. Qassem claimed that he was on the security detail that shuttled Zawahiri to one of Saddam's opulent palaces for a meeting with Saddam.

Both ABC News's *Nightline* and the PBS show *Wide Angle* also visited the prison and interviewed a "twenty-year veteran of Iraqi Intelligence" who told the same story. He was not named by *Wide Angle*; *Nightline* identified him only by a nom de guerre, Abu Aman Amaleeki. "In 1992, elements of al Qaeda came to Baghdad and met with Saddam Hussein," Amaleeki said. "And among them was Ayman al Zawahiri." Amaleeki later claimed, "I was present when Ayman al Zawahiri visited Baghdad."

These well-documented connections between Saddam and international terrorists—including a wide range of Islamic radicals—were widely ignored before the most recent war in Iraq. While it's true that these examples are more than a decade old, they have a direct bearing on the current debate about Iraq's links to al Qaeda and its affiliates. They shift the debate from the hypothetical to the empirical. The question, then, is not:

Would Saddam team up with Islamic terrorists? He did. The pertinent questions are these: Did Saddam Hussein continue or perhaps expand his relationships with these groups? And did the Islamic terrorists reciprocate?

The answer to both questions is the same: Yes.

CHAPTER FOUR

SADDAM AND OSAMA STRIKE BACK

Saddam's history of support for terrorists and the Iraqi attacks throughout the Gulf War clearly demonstrate his willingness to use terrorism to pursue goals he could not achieve through diplomacy or conventional war. Skeptics argue that this Iraqi terror came in the heat of the Iran-Iraq War and the Gulf War. But Saddam's use of terror didn't cease with the end of these conflicts.

Saddam believed that the war never ended. He has said so repeatedly since 1991. American and British bombers enforcing the no-fly zones established at the end of the Gulf War were continuing the Western "aggression" against Iraq. The United Nations sanctions imposed after that war, he argued, were tantamount to "terrorism" and "genocide" against the Iraqi people. At least once in 1993—and some experts believe twice—the Iraqi dictator used terror to avenge his embarrassing military defeat or, in his mind, to continue the war against America.

On January 14, 1993, six days before President George H. W. Bush would leave office, his successor gave an interview to Tom Friedman, of the *New York Times*. President-elect Bill Clinton startled many observers by seeming to reverse his previously hawkish position on Saddam. Although he supported ongoing strikes to punish Saddam for his continued intransigence, Friedman wrote, Clinton also "indicated that he was ready for a fresh start with President Saddam Hussein." "I always tell everybody I am a Baptist," said Clinton. "I believe in deathbed conversions. If he wants a different relationship with the United States and the United Nations, all he has to do is change his behavior." The following day, Clinton attempted to clarify his position by telling reporters that he supported the Bush administration's policies on Iraq. But the damage was done.

"The body language from Clinton toward Saddam Hussein was clear," says a senior official in the current Bush administration. "You've got a clean slate."

Although Saddam had celebrated when Bush lost to Clinton in November, the defeat did nothing to satisfy his appetite for retribution. Days after Clinton's conciliatory comments, Izzat Ibrahim al Douri, one of Saddam's top aides, addressed a session of the Popular Islamic Conference at Baghdad's National Theater. Reporter Mark Fineman from the *Los Angeles Times* was at the gathering and filed a story about it on January 26, 1993. "There are delegates from the most committed Islamic organizations on Earth," he wrote, "Afghan mujahideen (holy warriors), Palestinian militants, Sudanese fundamentalists, the Islamic Brotherhood and Pakistan's Party of Islam." In keeping with the spirit of the occasion, al Douri spoke in language his guests would appreciate. "We are blessed in this country for having the Islamic holy warrior Saddam

Hussein as a leader, who is guiding the country in a religious holy war against the infidels and nonbelievers."

Newsweek's Christopher Dickey, who covered the conference in 1993, described it in a column nearly a decade later, on September 9, 2002. "Islamic radicals from all over the Middle East, Africa, and Asia converged on Baghdad to show their solidarity with Iraq in the face of American aggression," he recalled. One speaker praised "the mujahed Saddam Hussein, who is leading this nation against the nonbelievers. Everyone has a task to do, which is to go against the American state." Al Douri told the crowd, "Our stand can now lead us to final victory, to Paradise."

Dickey wrote: "Every time I hear diplomats and politicians, whether in Washington or the capitals of Europe, declare that Saddam Hussein is a 'secular Baathist ideologue' who has nothing to do with Islamists or terrorist calls to jihad, I think of that afternoon and I wonder what they're talking about. If that was not a fledgling Qaeda itself at the Rashid convention, it sure was Saddam's version of it."

U.S. intelligence officials who have studied the Baghdad gatherings agree. The Islamic conferences were not just another of Saddam's attempts to ingratiate himself with the fundamentalists. According to several U.S. officials, the summits were crawling with Iraqi intelligence agents recruiting these radicals to help fight a terror war against the West.

"Real evil is hard to imagine," Dickey wrote, recalling the gathering. "Reasonable people do not want to recognize it, even when it stares them in the face; easier to listen to those who tell us that Saddam couldn't possibly see eye to eye with

Islamic fundamentalists and couldn't possibly be so foolish as to entrust them with weapons of mass destruction."

On January 17, 1993, the two-year anniversary of the start of the Gulf War, Saddam again signaled his refusal to cooperate with UN weapons inspectors, flouting the terms he had agreed to at the end of the Gulf War. Dozens of U.S. Tomahawk missiles obliterated sites of strategic importance to Iraq's continued weapons of mass destruction programs. Saddam Hussein, in a speech on Iraqi television, warned that "the day of battle has come." The language of jihad was unmistakable.

In the name of God, the most merciful, the most passionate, all great people, those who are satisfying the nation with glory and Jihad, the sons of our Arab glorious nation, the failures have come back again to Baghdad. They have come back to the steadfast Baghdad, the symbol of every noble city. And they have come back to the City of God the Greatest, bearing with them the failure that they have encountered which has run for all their previous trials, which started two years back until the day of the turning back on the 13th of this month . . .

Attack them, our beloved people. You are the glory of our nation. Attack them. God, his prophets, and his angels and his soldiers are standing beside you. Attack because this is the day of defense, where we'll see the sun which will never fade from it in order that it will be, and all Arabs and faithful people will be at the grade which God has bestowed upon them in the great side with their faith which is ceaseless and everlasting glory in the past, present, and future, the doors of which are open to all glory. Here our souls will be satisfied.

Saddam threatened revenge even if the allied bombing ended. "This is the new chapter in the Mother of all Battles," he said. "If the enemy continues its military aggression, or even if it stops, it is the final and decisive chapter which will be the end of all chapters." He was emphatic about the last point: "The Mother of all Battles is not the past."

Dickey remembered the Popular Islamic Conference six weeks after it ended, upon hearing "that a truck bomb had been detonated on the second level of the World Trade Center parking basement, with the aim of bringing one tower crashing down on the other . . . What struck me first about the bombing in 1993 was the date: February 26, exactly two years to the day after Desert Storm forced Saddam to make the humiliating announcement on Baghdad radio that he was withdrawing from Kuwait, even though his soldiers had 'performed their jihad duty.'"

Dickey wasn't the only one to make that association, and the date of the first World Trade Center bombing wasn't the only connection to Iraq. Laurie Mylroie, a former professor at Harvard and the U.S. Naval War College and an Iraq adviser to Bill Clinton's 1992 campaign, examined possible Iraqi involvement in the plot in her 2000 book, *A Study of Revenge*.

Her central thesis—that the main perpetrator of the bombings, Ramzi Yousef, was an agent of Iraq intelligence—requires several critical assumptions and is certainly open to debate. But the book raised several interesting questions. Why did

Yousef's friends in the United States call him "Rashid the Iraqi"? Another conspirator, Mohammed Salameh, made forty-six phone calls to Iraq two months before another conspirator arrived from Baghdad. His bill for June 1992 totaled $1,401. His phone was subsequently cut off for nonpayment, and with it, the ability of investigators to retrace his calls. Investigators determined that some of those calls went to a Baghdad-based intelligence operative for a neighboring country. Why did Salameh call this man? What is the likelihood that the Iraqi Intelligence Service was unaware of the communications? Who else did Salameh call? His uncle was a senior operative in the Baghdad office of the Iraqi government–supported Palestinian Liberation Organization. Was young Mohammed just checking in? Or was he receiving instructions?

More than a decade later, these remain open questions. But with the fall of the regime in Iraq, U.S. investigators have finally begun to get answers about the activities of another bomber, Abdul Rahman Yasin.

Yasin, an Iraqi who was born in Bloomington, Indiana, received a U.S. passport numbered 27082171 in Amman, Jordan, on June 21, 1992. He traveled from Baghdad to New Jersey in early September, approximately six months before the bombing, and moved into a modest apartment in Jersey City with his brother Musab Yasin and his mother.

At 12:18 P.M. on February 26, 1993, a van packed with explosives and cyanide exploded in the parking garage of the World Trade Center. Six people were killed and more than one thousand were injured in what was then the most devastating terrorist attack on American soil.

Yasin would later admit to mixing the chemicals for the bomb. In the process, he burned his leg, leaving a permanent scar. According to documents from the subsequent trial of several bombers, when the FBI searched Yasin's apartment days after the attack, they found residue from explosives on a scale and, in the trash, the pants he was wearing when he spilled the chemicals.

The FBI questioned Yasin twice. He disclaimed any significant role in the bombing and appeared cooperative, providing many details of the plot. So they let him go. In fact, FBI agents even drove him home after the interviews. On March 5, 1993, Yasin boarded a flight to Jordan. Upon arrival, he made his way to the Iraqi embassy in Amman and, with the urgent help of the embassy's second secretary, obtained Iraqi passport MO887925 under the name of Abdul Rahman S. Taher. He promptly returned to Baghdad. Within days, the FBI realized the magnitude of its mistake, but was powerless to correct it with Yasin safely in Iraq.

In its July 4, 1994 issue, *Newsweek* reported that there was "no question about Yasin's whereabouts": a reporter working for ABC and *Newsweek* had spotted him in Baghdad. ABC's *Day One* showed the Yasin family home, and neighbors told the reporter that Yasin "comes and goes freely" and visits his father there "almost daily." Most interesting, these neighbors said Yasin was "working for the Iraqi government."

The Iraqi regime approached the U.S. government with an offer to turn over Yasin.

"We informed the American government that we have important information about that event," said Tariq Aziz, Iraq's deputy prime minister, in a 2002 interview. An Iraqi representative told the State Department: "If you are interested, send a team to Baghdad to get that information."

The Iraqis did not claim, as they would years later, that Yasin had been jailed in Iraq. The offer to the State Department came with strings attached: the Iraqis wanted the U.S. government to sign a document absolving the Iraqi regime of any responsibility for the attacks. The Clinton administration refused.

Testimony from the trial of four accomplices in the bombing made clear that Yasin was not the bit player the FBI thought he was. He taught Mohammed Salameh how to drive the explosives-laden van. He was in frequent contact with conspirators outside the country and played a key role in obtaining the chemicals that made up the bomb.

The U.S. government received reports throughout the 1990s, mostly from defectors, that Yasin was living well in Iraq. But in an interview conducted by PBS *Frontline* on October 29, 2001, Mohammed al Douri, then Iraq's UN ambassador, denied any knowledge of Yasin's whereabouts.

Frontline confronted al Douri with reports that Yasin had been living in Iraq.

> AL DOURI: To my knowledge, he is not. To my knowledge, he is not, and there is no any relation with him. He is an American citizen, to my knowledge. We deny these allegations completely.
>
> *FRONTLINE*: He phoned the United States from Baghdad. He was there.
>
> AL DOURI: I do not know about that. I know nothing, really.
>
> *FRONTLINE*: You don't know whether he's there or not?

AL DOURI: Absolutely. I know that there is no relation with that guy, absolutely.

FRONTLINE: So someone just made that up?

AL DOURI: Absolutely . . . We have no relations with these kinds of guys, with all persons who are involved with terrorism. . .

Eight months later, on June 2, 2002, the Iraqi government changed its story. Tariq Aziz told Lesley Stahl of *60 Minutes* that the Iraqi government did, in fact, know where Yasin had been since his return to Baghdad: in a Mukhabarat prison.

According to Aziz, Yasin was sent back to Iraq after the bombing as part of a U.S. government-backed conspiracy to blame Iraq for the attack.

TARIQ AZIZ: Well, first of all, I have to tell you that we fear that sending Yasin back to Iraq after arresting him and interrogating him—interrogating him was a sting operation.

STAHL: You—you thought that the Americans were trying to sting you by sending him back?

AZIZ: Yes. Yes.

STAHL: But for what purpose?

AZIZ: To tell people later on that, "Look, this man who participated in that event now is in Iraq, etc.," and use it as they are doing now, using many false pretext, you see, to hurt Iraq in their own way.

STAHL: To win—to suggest that Iraq was involved in the bombing.

AZIZ: Yes. Yes.

Aziz also told Stahl that in October 2001 the Iraqis had again tried to turn Yasin over to the Americans. Bush administration sources would not talk specifically about the offer but confirmed the basic outlines of the Iraqi diplomat's story.

The offer in 2001 was not unlike the one seven years earlier. The Iraqis once again conditioned their offer on the U.S. government's signing a "receipt" clearing the Iraqi government of any role in the 1993 World Trade Center attack. With many unanswered questions about potential Iraqi complicity in the attacks, the Bush administration, like its predecessor, rejected the offer.

Aziz was not the only Iraqi Stahl interviewed for her report. Just as the debate about extending the War on Terror to Iraq heated up in the spring of 2002, the Iraqis made Yasin available to Stahl.

In an interview broadcast on June 2, 2002, Yasin confessed to his role in the conspiracy. He claimed he was a simple man in the United States for medical treatment who allowed himself to be manipulated by Ramzi Yousef, the mastermind of the bombing. They met, Yasin said, because they happened to live in the same building. "We used to drink tea together. My mother used to cook for the young men, lunch and dinner, Arabic food."

Yasin claimed that Yousef and Salameh, the conspirator who frequently telephoned Baghdad, politicized him. "They used to tell me that, 'You are an Iraqi and you have seen the destruction in Iraq.' And they used to tell me how Arabs suffered a great deal and that we have to send a message that this is not right. This is to revenge for my Palestinian brothers and my brothers in Saudi Arabia."

Yasin admitted to Stahl that he had evaluated bombing targets with Yousef and Salameh, that he had purchased the chemicals for the attack and helped create the bomb. He showed Stahl the scars on his leg from the chemicals that spilled as he mixed them for the explosion.

He also said that he and Yousef had originally targeted Jewish neighborhoods in Brooklyn before settling on the World Trade Center. "The majority of the people who work in the World Trade Center are Jews," Yasin explained.

When Stahl told Yasin that many Muslims also worked in the World Trade Center, the Iraqi apologized.

"I'm very sorry for what happened. I don't know what to do to make it up. My father died because of pain and sadness. It caused many troubles. I don't know how to apologize for it."

After the United States–led invasion on March 19, 2003, Yasin went on the run. U.S. intelligence officials in Iraq say they have come close to capturing him on several occasions. Although they haven't found him, Iraqis working with the coalition in Tikrit found a large cache of documents that mention his name.

The papers appear to be financial records kept by the former Iraqi regime, and they reveal that, contrary to the claims of top Iraqi officials, Yasin was not locked up upon his return to Iraq. Quite the opposite. The documents, produced by the Iraqi Intelligence Service, show that Yasin lived freely and received regime-financed housing and a monthly living stipend.

U.S. intelligence officials point out that there is no indication in the documents that the Iraqi regime financed Yasin before the 1993 World Trade Center attacks. Still, the support Yasin received continued until shortly before the war in Iraq, thus putting Saddam Hussein in direct violation of the warning President Bush issued on September 20, 2001: "From this day forward, any nation that continues to harbor or support terrorism will be regarded by the United States as a hostile regime."

Based on the regime's support for Yasin alone, Iraq qualified.

Official U.S. government inquiries have not turned up hard evidence of Iraqi involvement in the 1993 World Trade Center bombing. But several intelligence experts who have examined the evidence, including the late Jim Fox, head of the FBI's New York office at the time of the bombing, and James Woolsey, CIA director under President Clinton from 1993 to 1995, have concluded that Iraq had a hand in the attack.

If there remains significant disagreement about whether Iraq played a role in those attacks, the same cannot be said for another terrorist operation that took place a little more than one month later.

In March 1993, Wali al Ghazali, a male nurse from Najaf, was approached by a Mukhabarat officer named Abdel Hussein, who instructed Ghazali to report the following day to the intelligence office in Basra. He did as he was told.

Ghazali met with another agent, Abu Mrouwah, who gave him a surprising and dangerous mission: deliver the bomb that would kill President George H. W. Bush on his upcoming trip to Kuwait. Ghazali would later say Mrouwah told him to assassinate Bush because the former president was "Iraq's enemy number one and the cause of the economic embargo imposed on Iraq, and that it was a national duty."

On the surface, Ghazali was an unlikely choice. He was a

quiet man, a Shiite who had participated in the short-lived uprising against Saddam's regime after the Gulf War. He had never had any known association with Iraqi intelligence, except that he escaped its brutal punishment after the rebellion.

For the Iraqi regime, all this made Ghazali a perfect assassin. And there was one other important qualification: Ghazali had lost several family members during the allied bombing in the Gulf War. Those who survived remained in Iraq at the mercy of Saddam's intelligence services, who routinely tortured and killed relatives of those who defied the regime.

Ghazali gave the regime the one thing that might ensure its survival after the bombing: deniability. Whether he was captured or died in a suicide attack, the world would come to know him as an anti-Saddam agitator who simply wanted to avenge the losses he had suffered two years earlier. Perfect.

Several days later, another Iraqi intelligence agent named Mohammed Jawad contacted Raad Assadi to help with the operation. Assadi, a sometime informant for the Iraqi Intelligence Service who operated the Marbed coffee shop in Basra, made his money bootlegging liquor from Iraq to Kuwait, where it is strictly prohibited. If there was an expert in surreptitiously crossing the Iraq-Kuwait border, it was Assadi.

Not long after midnight on April 13, 1993, Ghazali and Assadi crossed unnoticed from Iraq into Kuwait. They took with them nine other Iraqis, several of whom simply wanted a ride to Kuwait and were apparently oblivious to the real purpose of the trip. Assadi himself would later say that he was not initially told that his companion was to kill President Bush, only that they were to plant bombs near malls and car dealerships to embarrass the Kuwaitis in front of their high-profile visitor.

Ghazali, he said, revealed the rest of the plot only after they had made it safely to Kuwait.

Under the floorboards of their vehicle, a Toyota Land Cruiser, sat nearly two hundred pounds of explosives. Before leaving Iraq for Kuwait, Ghazali received extensive instruction from Iraqi Intelligence on the timing devices for the bomb. He was also given several hand grenades, photographs of the planned bombing site at Kuwait University, a forged passport identifying him as a citizen of the United Arab Emirates, $1,100 in cash, and, in the event the car bomb malfunctioned, a "suicide belt" packed with explosives.

Ghazali and his accomplices parked the Land Cruiser and the second vehicle, a Chevrolet Suburban, at a sheep farm owned by a Kuwaiti smuggler named Bader Jiyad Shimmeri on the outskirts of Kuwait City. They headed downtown to an apartment Shimmeri kept in the city. That night, according to Kuwaiti court documents, they drank whiskey, watched television, and chatted.

The would-be assassins were unaware of two important developments since their plot was hatched. The event honoring President Bush for liberating Kuwait had been moved from its original location. More important, Kuwaiti authorities had received a tip about the alleged smugglers and discovered a bag containing materials for the bomb.

On April 14, police raided the residence at the sheep farm, discovered the vehicles and the whiskey, and arrested several members of the large group. Ghazali and Assadi, the two Iraqis who had received the orders from Iraqi intelligence, returned to the farm from downtown Kuwait and spotted the police activity. The fled back to the city, where they spent the night.

The next day, Ghazali and Assadi stole a Mercedes and attempted to return to Iraq. But they filled it with the wrong type of gasoline, rendering the getaway car inoperable. They were apprehended later that day as they walked toward the Iraqi border.

Kuwaiti police at first had no idea that they had foiled an assassination attempt. They failed to uncover the bomb in their initial searches of the Land Cruiser. After three days in detention, Assadi told the Kuwaitis about the bomb, leading some observers to speculate that he had been tortured to induce a confession.

That the CIA was dubious upon learning about the plot was understandable, since it was disclosed not by the Kuwaitis but in an Arabic-language newspaper in London. Investigators were convinced, however, when they examined the bomb, which bore a strong resemblance to explosives planted by Iraq during the Gulf War. Both Ghazali and Assadi confessed to the crime. "I have been pushed by people who had no mercy," said Ghazali on the first day of his trial. "So now I'm asking for your mercy and the mercy of the Kuwaiti people. You know I fear the Iraqi regime, the Iraqi regime pushed me."

President Clinton received the findings of the FBI and the CIA on June 24, 1993. Two days later, he ordered air strikes on the Iraqi intelligence headquarters. Clinton explained the decision in an address to the nation.

[T]here is compelling evidence that there was, in fact, a plot to assassinate former President Bush; and that this plot, which included the use of a powerful bomb made in Iraq, was directed and pursued by the Iraqi Intelligence Service.

We should not be surprised by such deeds, coming as they do from a regime like Saddam Hussein's . . . Saddam has repeatedly violated the will and conscience of the international community.

But this attempt at revenge by a tyrant against the leader of the world coalition that defeated him in war is particularly loathsome and cowardly. . . .

Saddam Hussein has demonstrated repeatedly that he will resort to terrorism or aggression if left unchecked. Our intent was to target Iraq's capacity to support violence against the United States and other nations, and to deter Saddam Hussein from supporting such outlaw behavior in the future. Therefore, we directed our action against the facility associated with Iraq's support of terrorism, while making every effort to minimize the loss of innocent life.

Defense Secretary Les Aspin explained further: "The assassination attempt was not an act of a small group of people acting independently," he said. "The evidence is very conclusive that it was the work of the Iraqi Intelligence Service and is an action that would have had to have been approved by the highest levels of the Iraqi government."

Twenty-three Tomahawk missiles targeted the Iraqi Intelligence Service headquarters. "The primary agency responsibility" of the Iraqi Intelligence Service, Aspin said, is "for terrorist attacks abroad, as it tried to do in this case."

The following day, U.S. ambassador to the United Nations Madeleine Albright shared the evidence—including photographs of the bombs—with the Security Council. "Certain aspects of these devices have been found only in devices linked

to Iraq and not in devices used by any other terrorist groups."
In background interviews with reporters, top Clinton administration officials claimed that there were indications that Saddam Hussein personally ordered the attack.

"Even after President Clinton signaled a new era in U.S.-
Iraqi relations, Saddam tries to murder the [former] president
of the United States," says a senior official in the current Bush
administration. "That means one of two things. Either he was
trying to show his people that he wouldn't back down or that
he wanted revenge."

And Iraq initially promised revenge for the attack on Iraqi
Intelligence Service headquarters. "We will pursue anyone who
dares to attack our dear Iraq and severely punish these evil in-
sects," said Saber Abdul Aziz al Douri, the head of Iraqi intelligence. Tariq Aziz later backed away from these bellicose
comments.

Vice President Al Gore defended the strikes and took Clinton's rhetoric several steps further. "The suffering inside Iraq
can come to an end when Saddam Hussein's regime is replaced," said Gore. "And I hope—and most of the world community hopes—that this regime based on terrorism and
atrocities against his own people will be replaced. Over time,
we hope to achieve that result."

CHAPTER FIVE

A HOME FOR TERROR

Three years before American politicians like Al Gore began advocating regime change in Iraq, a series of unsettling political developments in the Sudan created fertile ground for future collaboration between Saddam Hussein and Osama bin Laden.

In the summer of 1989, Hassan al Turabi, Sudan's foreign minister, called for jihad and announced that Sudan would soon be under Islamic rule. On June 30, a small group of high-ranking officials from the Sudanese Army informed Prime Minister Sadiq al Madhi, who had been democratically elected three years earlier, that his services were no longer needed.

None of this was clear at the time. Although a coup had been anticipated, no one recognized it as it happened. Accounts in the Western press were maddeningly vague. A general chronology was all that was available: Several officials from the previous government had been jailed, and Lieutenant General Omar Hassan al Bashir, a relatively unknown former battlefield commander, assumed power. Adding to the confusion was the fact that the man many suspected of plotting the coup, Hassan al Turabi, was imprisoned with his former colleagues.

In time, Turabi was released. He boasted of his critical behind-the-scenes role in orchestrating the ouster and, within weeks, settled in comfortably as Bashir's number two. With the coup, Turabi took an important first step toward achieving his stated goal of establishing fundamentalist Islamic governments throughout the Middle East and North Africa.

Sudan seemed like a good place to start. The largely Muslim state had been torn apart by a lengthy civil war between Islamic radicals in the north and the Christians and animists in the south. Sudan's non-Muslims together with a minority of moderate Muslims had objected to the imposition of some elements of *sharia*, or Islamic law, but Turabi answered those protests with an even stricter Islamic regime.

Thin and frail, with dark skin and a white beard, Turabi hardly looks like the ruler of a nation where the strongest survive. He wears long, flowing white robes that match his turban and large brown glasses that are too big for his head.

But those familiar with Turabi and his philosophy portray him as a smooth operator who shifts seamlessly from diplomatic language designed to please the West to the incendiary rhetoric of the fiercest jihadist. Educated at the University of London and the Sorbonne in Paris, he is also a true believer in the inevitability of a radical Islamic revival.

As the power behind Bashir, Sudan's titular leader for much of the 1990s, Turabi hastened the country's transition from hapless failed state to dangerous terrorist haven. Shortly after seizing power, Turabi's National Islamic Front waived visa requirements for all Arabs—a not-so-subtle invitation to terrorists unwanted in their native lands.

In one of his first high-profile moves on the international stage, Turabi embraced Saddam Hussein on the eve of the Gulf War. In the days after Iraq's invasion of Kuwait, Turabi met with Saddam at least twice, according to his cousin Mudawi Turabi.

On October 1, 1990, Hassan al Turabi led a diverse delegation of forty Islamic fundamentalist leaders to Jordan for a meeting with representatives from the Iraqi regime. According to a top secret CIA report published internally on June 21, 2002, called "Iraq and al Qaeda: Interpreting a Murky Relationship," an FBI source said that a bin Laden envoy was there, as were the leaders of the Muslim Brotherhood in Jordan. Turabi, who served as the meeting's spokesman, announced that Hussein had pledged to release prominent clerics who had been held by his regime. Saddam, who at one time was a leading advocate of secularism, also promised to incorporate elements of Islamic law into the Iraqi legal code.

Following his meeting with the Iraqis, Turabi held a press conference on October 1, 1990, to advise Muslims of their duty to undertake "a struggle—or jihad, if you want to use the Arabic word—to protect their territories and their holy land and their wealth." He then turned his comments to the West. In the event of war, Turabi warned, "there is going to be all forms of jihad all over the world because it is an issue of foreign troops on sacred soil." When he was asked to clarify his statement, Turabi said there would be "demonstrations, fighting, targeting the enemy everywhere."

"In every place, it is division and the absence of an Islamic order which is leading to these conflicts," Turabi said.

The Islamists' embrace of the secular Iraqi leader was not without anxiety. "Many of us naturally, as Arabs, oppose the presence of foreign troops on Arab land so soon after our freedom from foreign occupation," an unnamed leader of the Muslim Brotherhood told the *New York Times* on October 4, 1990. "And as Muslims, we oppose the presence of nonbelievers near our shrines. But we cannot, after all these years of Saddam's suppression of Islamists, feel happy about an association with him."

Happy or not, the Islamists, led by Hassan al Turabi, did indeed associate with Saddam. One of the early meetings came when Ayman al Zawahiri, "the Doctor," traveled to Baghdad for a visit with Saddam. As noted, one Iraqi intelligence officer captured by Kurdish forces before the most recent war in Iraq provided security for Zawahiri. Another meeting, this one in the Sudan, was mentioned in a top secret memo from undersecretary of defense Douglas J. Feith to the Senate Intelligence Committee on October 27, 2003.

According to a May 2003 debriefing of a senior Iraqi intelligence officer, Iraqi intelligence established a highly secretive relationship with Egyptian Islamic Jihad, and later with al Qaeda. The first meeting in 1992 between the Iraqi Intelligence Service (IIS), and al Qaeda was brokered by al Turabi. Former IIS deputy director Faruq Hijazi and senior al Qaeda leader Zawahiri were at the meeting—the first of several between 1992 and 1995 in Sudan. Additional meetings between Iraqi intelligence and al Qaeda were held in Pakistan. Members of al Qaeda would sometimes visit Baghdad where they would meet the Iraqi intelligence chief in a safe house. The report claimed that Saddam insisted the relationship with al Qaeda be kept secret.

A foreign intelligence service that has provided information generally assessed as reliable would later inform the CIA that Hijazi provided al Qaeda blank Yemeni passports in 1992. The meeting brokered by Turabi may have provided Hijazi with that opportunity.

After his rise to power in the Sudan, Hassan al Turabi quickly became something of a fixture in CIA reporting on international terrorism. As soon as he opened Sudanese borders, a steady flow of mujahideen fighters, ragtag leftovers from the Afghan resistance to the Soviet Union in the 1980s, made their way to Khartoum. Among those fighters was Osama bin Laden. The close relationship between al Qaeda and the Sudanese government was born.

While bin Laden and Turabi can both be classified as "Islamic radicals," they had different ideas about the role of Islam in the modern world. Bin Laden was an ascetic who longed for a return to the past glories of Islam. Turabi, too, argued forcefully for a strict interpretation of the Koran, but unlike bin Laden, he believed that Islam and modernity were not mutually exclusive.

Despite this important difference, bin Laden and Turabi had other crucial things in common. They both predicted an Islamic revival, and they both denounced the presence of U.S. troops, infidels in uniform, on Arab "sacred lands." They sought and won the cooperation of radical Shiites ruling Iran despite deep ideological differences. And they were both willing to work with almost anyone to advance their vision of Islam, including ostensibly secular leaders.

Perhaps most important, both men saw Sudan as their opportunity, finally, to create an Islamic state that would enforce *sharia*, or Islamic law. More worrisome to many Western observers was Turabi's dogged effort to fold secular Arab nationalists, like Saddam Hussein, into his more radical fundamentalist ideology. The Sudanese strongman appealed to the practical instincts of secular nationalists.

"Arab nationalists know they must come home, since they have no future with the masses," Turabi told the *New York Times* on May 31, 1992. "Islam is becoming temporal. You in the West had better get used to it, and you should not be afraid of it. We are not your enemy. Besides, objectively, the future is ours."

Within a few years, many of the world's most deadly terrorist organizations—each with its own agenda—began to shift some of their operations to Sudan. They included Abu Nidal Organization, Party of God, Islamic Holy War, Hamas, Hezbollah, Egyptian Islamic Jihad, and a fledgling al Qaeda. Turabi gave bin Laden's organization a base from which to operate and access to those things that only a state can provide—passports, visas, diplomatic pouches for secure international deliveries. In exchange, bin Laden gave him battle-hardened fighters for the civil war raging in Sudan, as well as a big bank account and construction equipment the poor African nation would use to rebuild its infrastructure. By early 1992, accounts in the Western press regularly referred to Sudan as a terrorist safe haven. The State Department dispatched an envoy to warn Turabi to stop supporting terrorists. It didn't work.

On December 5, 1992, former Sudanese labor minister George Logokwa, once a Turabi ally, told reporters that radicals had established seven terrorist training camps in and around Khartoum. Logokwa further alleged that Turabi's government had accepted $30 million from Iran for the camps, and that instruction was sometimes provided by members of the Iranian Revolution Guard.

This unlikely cooperation between Shiite and Sunni radicals, between Iran and bin Laden acolytes, was underscored in testimony that a senior al Qaeda leader gave in a U.S. court on October 20, 2000. Ali Mohamed, a senior Egyptian Islamic Jihad terrorist who began working for bin Laden in 1991, pleaded guilty to several terrorism-related charges, including helping to plan the 1998 embassy bombings in Kenya and Tanzania. He received a reduced sentence for cooperating with American authorities.

> I was aware of certain contacts between al Qaeda and [Egyptian Islamic] al Jihad, on one side, and Iran and Hezbollah on the other side. I arranged security for a meeting in the Sudan between [Emad] Mughaniyah, Hezbollah's chief, and bin Laden. Hezbollah provided explosives training for al Qaeda and al Jihad. Iran supplied Egyptian Jihad with weapons. Iran also used Hezbollah to supply explosives that were disguised to look like rocks.

Even as he cultivated ties with Iran's governing radicals, Turabi sought to build his relationship with their longtime nemesis, Saddam Hussein. In the aftermath of Iraq's humiliating defeat in the Gulf War, Turabi assumed the chief role in bringing Saddam and Osama bin Laden together. Taking baby steps before big ones, he proposed a nonaggression pact between the two natural enemies. The Feith memo summarized a report from the CIA this way:

> According to CIA reporting in 1993, National Islamic Front (NIF) leader Hassan al-Turabi helped bin Laden develop a relationship with Iraq. Bin Laden wanted to expand his organization's capabilities through ties with Iraq. In a finished report (Al Qaeda in Sudan 1992–1996), CIA maintained that in 1991 Iraq sought Sudan's assistance to establish links to al Qaeda. At al-Turabi's urging, Bin Laden developed an "understanding" in 1994 with Saddam not to support any anti-Saddam activities. The same source reported that Iraq and Bin Laden agreed to cooperate on unspecified activities.

The Pentagon had its own reporting indicating the significance of Turabi's role as intermediary. A senior Iraqi intelligence official was interrogated in Stuttgart, Germany, at the Joint Interrogation Center System, a collaborative effort between the United States, Germany, France, and Britain. German officials handled the interrogation and "an experienced U.S. intelligence officer with native Arabic capability participated in the source's debriefing for this report. According to the field report, the US debriefer's initial assessment of source is that he seems credible."

According to DOD reporting, a former Iraqi intelligence officer with direct access to reported information said al-Turabi was instrumental in arranging the Iraqi–al Qaeda relationship. The defector said Iraq sought al Qaeda influence, through its connections with Afghanistan, to facilitate the transshipment of proscribed weapons and equipment to Iraq. In return, Iraq provided al Qaeda with training and instructors. This DOD source corroborates the CIA report that al-Turabi helped broker a relationship between bin Laden and the Iraqi regime.

The National Security Agency (NSA), the branch of the U.S. intelligence community that specializes in intercepting communications, corroborated this reporting in a finding it distributed to the intelligence community in February 2003.

The intelligence on Turabi comes from three different sources and was reported by three different agencies—the CIA, the Defense Department, and the NSA.

The information on the nascent relationship between Saddam's regime and bin Laden reveals another crucial detail: the outreach went both ways. Bin Laden "wanted to expand his organization's capabilities through ties with Iraq," and Saddam "sought al Qaeda influence, through its connections with Afghanistan, to facilitate" the shipment of weapons and equipment banned under UN sanctions.

Initially, bin Laden had to overcome internal resistance to his overtures with Saddam. The CIA referred to these battles inside the "Islamic Army," the agency's name for bin Laden's group throughout the early and mid-1990s, in a report published May 14, 2002. The Feith memo summarized the report.

A CIA report from a contact with good access[,] some of whose reporting has been corroborated[,] said that certain elements in the "Islamic Army" of Bin Laden were against the secular regime of Saddam. Overriding the internal factional strife that was developing, Bin Laden came to an "understanding" with Saddam that the Islamic Army would no longer support anti-Saddam activities.

The memo noted that the source's credibility was open to question, but during the legal proceedings that followed the 1998 embassy bombings, al Qaeda members furnished corroborating statements: "According to sensitive reporting released in US court documents during the African Embassy trial, in 1993 Bin Laden reached an 'understanding' with Saddam under which he (bin Laden) forbade al Qaeda operations to be mounted against the Iraqi leader."

These trials, along with the numerous debriefings that preceded them, would provide American investigators, intelligence officials, and terrorism scholars a new window into the strategy and tactics of al Qaeda during its tenure in Sudan. The key witness for the U.S. government was Jamal Ahmed al Fadl, a founding member of al Qaeda who was for years one of bin Laden's most trusted deputies. Among the duties he listed were running al Qaeda front companies; arranging assistance for al Qaeda affiliate groups from the Philippines, Lebanon, Tajikistan, Pakistan, and elsewhere; making sure the Sudanese government repaid its debts to al Qaeda; planning assassination attempts on political opponents of the ruling Sudanese political party, the National Islamic Front; and attempting to obtain uranium for bin Laden.

Al Fadl left al Qaeda after its leaders discovered that he was not reporting commissions he took for conducting financial transactions for the group. The substance of his reporting is widely believed to be credible. Two of the revelations in the testimony stood out: the extent to which al Qaeda and the Sudanese government overlapped, at times becoming almost indistinguishable, and bin Laden's unwavering determination to obtain weapons of mass destruction.

Al Fadl said bin Laden dispatched him to Sudan in 1991. Bin Laden had become enamored of Turabi and, despite the objections of some of his chief lieutenants, had decided to move al Qaeda operations to Sudan. Al Fadl, instructed to scout out the country, was given $250,000 by Ayman al Zawahiri, who was at the time running Egyptian Islamic Jihad and working closely with al Qaeda. Zawahiri told al Fadl to buy farms that al Qaeda could turn into terrorist training camps. According to al Fadl's testimony, given in broken English, the Sudanese intelligence service was working with al Qaeda even before bin Laden and Zawahiri arrived in the country.

> I remember the Egyptian Jihad Group, they got training inside the farm. And the explosive make noise, and the residential not far from the farm, and they complain about that and they go to the local police and tell them it's a big noise comes from the farm. And the police come to the farm, but we call the intelligence office because we have relationship with them, and the intelligence office came and they tell the local police "we take care of that" and "don't worry about that." And they take us to the jail and they say,

"you shouldn't do that, we tell you to refresh, not to make real explosives."

In an exchange with Patrick Fitzgerald, a U.S. attorney, al Fadl described a meeting with bin Laden in an al Qaeda guesthouse in 1992.

> AL FADL: We asked him if we have to make money because the business is very bad in Sudan, because the pounds go down and the dollar is strong. The Sudanese pounds always go weak against the dollar.
>
> FITZGERALD: What if anything did bin Laden say?
>
> AL FADL: He say our agenda is bigger than business. We not going to make business here, but we need to help the government and the government help our group, and this is our purpose.

The Sudanese government helped al Qaeda almost immediately by creating two hundred Sudanese passports for al Qaeda members. Al Qaeda was equally useful to his hosts: al Fadl explained that the Sudanese government commissioned bin Laden's Hijra Construction company to build a road connecting the capital, Khartoum, with several other cities throughout the country. In late 1993, the government continued the cycle by giving bin Laden the government-owned Khartoum Tannery.

Al Qaeda also helped the National Islamic Front procure equipment and weaponry for the ongoing civil war. Al Fadl testified that al Qaeda gave assistance to Defaa al Shabi, a division of the Sudanese Army fighting the Christians in southern

Sudan. "We buy for them communications for the offices, and also like radio and telephone, and we also buy Kalashnikovs [Soviet-made rifles] for them."

The overlap between the Sudanese government and al Qaeda intensified when the National Islamic Front sent al Fadl to assassinate Sadiq al Madhi, the Sudanese prime minister ousted by Turabi, who had been speaking out against Turabi's National Islamic Front in Friday prayers and other public forums. Al Fadl was instructed to penetrate al Madhi's Umma Party. After meeting with the former president and asking him questions supplied by the National Islamic Front, al Fadl returned to brief Sudanese intelligence officials. Fitzgerald sought to clarify this testimony.

> FITZGERALD: Just so we are clear, the people asking you to kill Sadiq al Madhi were from the Islamic National Front and the intelligence service, not from al Qaeda?
> AL FADL: No, from Islamic National Front.

Al Fadl reported that assassinating al Madhi would be very difficult, and the plan was eventually aborted. His testimony about the strong relationship between Sudanese intelligence and al Qaeda was underscored later by separate testimony from Ali Mohamed, another top bin Laden deputy: "I went to the Sudan in 1994 to train bin Laden's bodyguards, security detail. I trained those conducting the security of the interior of his compound, and coordinated with the Sudanese intelligence agents who were responsible for the exterior security."

On cross-examination, al Fadl was asked directly about

Iraq. His answers suggest that if the West preferred to separate Iraq from Islamic fundamentalism, Osama bin Laden did not.

Al Qaeda leaders, he said, were angry that "the United States was killing Iraqis with their sanction," a point bin Laden himself has made in several of his public statements. Al Fadl further admitted that al Qaeda sought uranium to attack Americans in response to the situation in Iraq.

More to the point, defense attorney David Baugh asked al Fadl how al Qaeda leaders felt about Saddam. Al Fadl recalled bin Laden speaking out against Saddam in Afghanistan in 1988. Still, more than a decade later, al Fadl's responses reflected far more ambivalence.

BAUGH: Is Saddam Hussein liked or disliked by al Qaeda?
AL FADL: They don't think he's real government Muslim.
BAUGH: Do they like him or dislike him?
AL FADL: It's hard to say yes or no.

This seemingly evasive answer is in fact quite revealing. Surely if bin Laden and Saddam were the bitter enemies today's conventional wisdom suggests, such uncompromising foes that cooperation was all but impossible, it would not have been hard for al Fadl to "say yes or no." Al Qaeda's terror, al Fadl testified, was related to the situation in Iraq.

BAUGH: Am I correct, sir, that it was your position personally and al Qaeda's position that if enough Americans were killed they would stop bombing Iraq?
AL FADL: The al Qaeda people, yeah, they believed that.

The most terrifying aspect of al Fadl's testimony came when another defense attorney, David Stern, asked al Fadl about al Qaeda's pursuit of chemical weapons. Al Fadl described a series of trips he took with Mamdouh Salim, aka Abu Hajer al Iraqi. The work on chemical weapons took place at least three years before the CIA established an al Qaeda desk in 1996 and six years before the State Department placed al Qaeda on its list of terrorist organizations in 1999.

> STERN: And on some occasions you were even directly involved with weapons, weren't you?
> AL FADL: Yes.
> STERN: There came a time when you went to Helat Koko in Khartoum, remember that time?
> AL FADL: Yes.
> STERN: And you went there with Salim, didn't you?
> AL FADL: Yes.
> STERN: And when you went there, you were going to a place where they were making chemical weapons, right?
> AL FADL: Yes, that's what I told—they told me.
> STERN: And that's what you believed?
> AL FADL: Yes.

Al Fadl acknowledged that chemical weapons are used to kill people and testified that despite this knowledge, he continued to help al Qaeda obtain them.

> STERN: You continued to run your [al Qaeda] businesses?
> AL FADL: Yes.

STERN: You continued to have that money from your businesses go to do things, including chemical weapons, right?

AL FADL: Yes. Yes.

The reporting on Sudan's activities throughout the early 1990s—in both "open sources" and through clandestine intelligence gathering—presented a deeply troubling scenario. Under the permissive Sudanese regime, rogue states and terrorist groups with little in common other than their hatred of the West and the United States had begun to pool their resources. They included radical Islamic Sunnis, secular Sunnis, Arab Nationalists, and extremist Islamic Shiites.

Most ominous, Hassan al Turabi used his personal relationship with bin Laden to cultivate ties between the increasingly powerful al Qaeda leader and Saddam Hussein. And while there is no evidence that al Qaeda's early dabbling in weapons of mass destruction had its roots in Iraqi technology, their collaboration on those deadly arms was only a matter of time.

CHAPTER SIX

"THE FATHER AND GRANDFATHER OF TERRORISTS"

Active collaboration between al Qaeda and Iraqi intelligence started slowly, moving from indirect financial dealings and discussions of third-party arms transfers to Iraqi training of al Qaeda terrorists, perhaps including bin Laden himself.

In 1994, according to CIA reporting, Saddam and bin Laden shared an interest in an al Qaeda–linked Algerian terrorist organization, Groupe Islamique Armé. In the early 1990s, the GIA was one of the key affiliate groups in bin Laden's orbit. Thousands of mujahideen veterans from the Afghanistan war took up arms for the GIA in Algeria, with financial support from bin Laden and, apparently, the Iraqi regime.

"We were convinced money from Iraq was going to bin Laden, who was then sending it places Iraq wanted it to go," former CIA senior counterterrorism analyst Dr. Stanley Bedlington told *USA Today* on December 3, 2001. "There certainly is no doubt that Saddam Hussein had pretty strong ties to bin Laden while he was in Sudan, whether it was directly or through intermediaries. We traced considerable sums of money going from bin Laden to the GIA in Algeria. We believed some of the money came from Iraq."

Bedlington later elaborated on the relationship. Bin Laden–linked groups, he said, effectively served as money launderers for Saddam, who was then determined to circumvent the sanctions imposed on his country after the Gulf War. Each party that handled money took a cut. "Osama bin Laden had established contact with the GIA," says Bedlington. "Saddam was using bin Laden to ship funds to his own contacts through the GIA."

Using third parties obviously had its benefits and its risks. The use of intermediaries clearly widens the circle of individuals with knowledge of the relationship; it also makes such coordination more difficult to track. "One thing about terrorism that I learned early on," Bedlington says, "is that there is often a hand-off. It's never clear cut: 'X did this.'"

In one of the earliest known meetings between Iraqi intelligence and Osama bin Laden, the al Qaeda leader requested that Iraq serve as a go-between for arms shipments. The Feith memo summarized the debriefing of the deputy director of Iraqi intelligence.

During a May 2003 custodial interview with Faruq Hijazi, he said in a 1994 meeting with bin Laden in the Sudan, bin Laden requested that Iraq assist al Qaeda with the procurement of an unspecified number of Chinese-manufactured antiship limpet mines. Bin Laden thought that Iraq should be able to procure the mines through third-country intermediaries for ultimate delivery to al Qaeda. Hijazi said he was under orders from Saddam only to listen to bin

Laden's requests and then report back to him. Bin Laden also requested the establishment of al Qaeda training camps inside Iraq.

As noted, information obtained during debriefings from captured enemies, whether al Qaeda or Iraqi, should be treated with some degree of skepticism. Interrogators provide subjects with strong incentives to cooperate and make life miserable for those who don't. Information extracted from such interrogations is tested against previously collected intelligence and reporting from other sources. American officials familiar with Hijazi's interrogations say his reporting has been uneven. He confirmed and provided important details about his meetings with al Qaeda leadership in the early and mid-1990s, such as this one from 1994, but initially denied a series of contacts in 1998. Intelligence officials from the United States and the region are fairly certain, based on communications intercepts, that the meetings took place.

They also find Hijazi's account of the 1994 meeting generally credible, although they are uncertain of its precise timing. The CIA had previous reporting of a similar meeting, but believed it took place in 1995.

If Hijazi's portrayal of the meeting is accurate, bin Laden's request for antiship limpet mines from Iraq marks an important development in relations between Iraq and al Qaeda. His willingness to accept help from Saddam deflates the most stubborn myth about the Iraq–al Qaeda connection: Osama bin Laden would not work with an infidel like Saddam Hussein. It is unclear whether Saddam honored bin Laden's request. But with his appeal for help, bin Laden demonstrated that he was willing to upgrade the relationship from the informal nonaggression pact reached in 1993 to active collaboration.

Western and Arab intelligence sources believe Hijazi was among the Iraqi officials whose knowledge of the Saddam–bin Laden relationship was most intimate. U.S. intelligence documents refer to him as the "point man" for the connection. Hijazi's job as an emissary from Saddam to bin Laden spanned almost a decade and was reported throughout the late 1990s in both Western and Arabic-language press.

Bin Laden, too, had a high-ranking associate responsible for handling important aspects of the relationship. Abu Hajer al Iraqi had been with bin Laden since the founding of al Qaeda and had served on its leadership council as a religious instructor. Others in the group looked to him as an authority on Islam and recall his reciting lengthy passages from the Koran from memory. He also worked as a business manager and as al Qaeda's chief of technology, but his most important role was as al Qaeda's chief procurer of weapons of mass destruction. It was Abu Hajer al Iraqi who accompanied Jamal al Fadl, the U.S. government's witness in the 1998 embassy bombing trial, to a chemical weapons facility outside Khartoum in late 1993 or early 1994.

Like many bin Laden lieutenants, Abu Hajer was not particularly fond of Saddam. He was known to hold forth on the evils of the secular Iraqi dictator and told associates that he had prepared himself for his role as an al Qaeda leader by using Saddam's regime as a bad example. Bush administration officials speculate that bin Laden's fixation on obtaining WMD may have required Abu Hajer to disregard his personal views of Saddam. It's also possible that his meetings with Iraqi intelligence persuaded Abu Hajer that al Qaeda could work with Saddam.

Abu Hajer had had such a change of heart once before. When bin Laden was considering a move from Afghanistan to Sudan in the early 1990s, he dispatched Abu Hajer to meet with Hassan al Turabi. Abu Hajer had previously advised bin Laden against working with Turabi's group because they did not share the same objectives, but after meeting with representatives from Turabi's National Islamic Front, Abu Hajer reported to bin Laden that such disagreements could be overcome and that a move to Sudan was advisable.

Whatever the reason, Abu Hajer clearly changed his views with respect to Saddam. According to the 2002 CIA report, "Iraq and al Qaeda: Interpreting a Murky Relationship": "Mamdouh Mahmud Ahmed Salim, aka Abu Hajer al-Iraqi, a top al Qaeda logistician now jailed in the United States—had a good relationship with Iraqi intelligence and at some time before mid-1995 went on an al Qaeda mission to Iraq to discuss unspecified cooperation with the Iraqi government, according to FBI information."

U.S. intelligence officials suspect that Abu Hajer's 1995 trip to Iraq was just one in a series of meetings he had with Iraqi intelligence. The most worrisome prospect, according to several Bush administration officials, is that Abu Hajer sought Iraqi support for al Qaeda's fledgling weapons of mass destruction program. Western and Arab intelligence services had long suspected al Qaeda of seeking WMD. Bin Laden would later say that acquiring such weapons was a "religious duty" of Muslims.

Even skeptics of the connection concede that these high-level contacts between Iraqi intelligence and al Qaeda took place throughout the mid-1990s. "I'm unpersuaded by what I've seen so far that there was any kind of organizational link between Saddam and al Qaeda," says Winston Wiley, a high-ranking CIA official under both Democrat and Republican presidents. "But I wouldn't doubt that al Qaeda and Saddam had contacts."

According to a CIA senior executive memorandum dated September 13, 2002, "the most credible information" available to U.S. intelligence on bin Laden's contacts with Iraq came from a man referred to only as "the 1996 source," whom the CIA believes may have been a member of bin Laden's security detail or one of his drivers. The source apparently did not attend the substantive parts of bin Laden's meetings and was not in his inner circle. But a summary of the reporting from this source included in the Feith memo asserts that "the information and level of detail is so specific that this source's reports read almost like a diary. Specific dates of when bin Laden flew to various cities are included, as well as names of individuals he met."

Among those individuals was a top Iraqi explosives expert and his boss, the head of Iraqi intelligence. The reporting on those meetings, as related in the Pentagon's memo to the Senate Intelligence Committee, comes from a "well-placed source."

"Bin Laden was receiving training on bomb making from the IIS's [Iraqi Intelligence Service's] principal technical expert on making sophisticated explosives, Brigadier Salim al Ahmed. Brigadier Salim was observed at bin Laden's farm in Khartoum in Sept-Oct. 1995 and again in July 1996, in the company of the Director of Iraqi Intelligence, Mani-abd-al-Rashid-al-Tikriti."

And later more reporting, from the same "well-placed" source:

> The Director of Iraqi Intelligence, Mani-abd-al-Rashid-al-Tikriti, met privately with bin Laden at his farm in Sudan in July 1996. Tikriti used an Iraqi delegation traveling to Khartoum to discuss bilateral cooperation as his "cover" for his own entry into Sudan to meet with bin Laden and Hassan al-Turabi. The Iraqi intelligence chief and two other IIS [Iraqi Intelligence Service] officers met at bin Laden's farm and discussed bin Laden's request for IIS technical assistance in: (a) making letter and parcel bombs; (b) making bombs which could be placed on aircraft and detonated by changes in barometric pressure; and (c) making false passport [*sic*]. Bin Laden specifically requested that [Brigadier Salim al Ahmed], Iraqi intelligence's premier explosives maker—especially skilled in making car bombs—remain with him in Sudan. The Iraqi intelligence chief instructed Salim to remain in Sudan with bin Laden as long as required.

The claims, of course, are staggering. If true, these revelations point to a relationship far more intimate than the mere "contacts" reported by the U.S. intelligence committee throughout the 1990s.

But certain aspects of this reporting cry out for further explanation. A "well-placed source" is not necessarily the same thing as a credible source. Well-placed sources can, of course, provide useful details about the subjects of their reporting. They can also lie or exaggerate or simply make mistakes.

Also, the reported timing of the meeting, in July 1996, raises several questions. In response to pressure from the West, bin Laden was expelled from Sudan in May of that year, two months before he allegedly met in Khartoum with the head of Iraqi intelligence. In early July, bin Laden gave an interview to British journalist Robert Fisk in "a remote and desolate mountainous area of Afghanistan's Nongarhar province."

Following his expulsion, bin Laden kept close relations with Hassan al Turabi and his Islamist colleagues in Sudan, and al Qaeda maintained a strong presence there. It's not inconceivable that bin Laden returned to Sudan at some point in July, as the well-placed source reported, and met with the Iraqis. Perhaps the source provided the dates of travel, and such information was simply left out of the Pentagon memo.

Iraqi intelligence was also training "non-Iraqi Arabs" closer to home. The best-known of these training camps was the one at Salman Pak, approximately twenty miles south of Baghdad. The terrorism schools were highly secretive—known only to those who worked inside them and officials at the highest levels of Saddam's regime.

Sabah Khodada, a former captain in the Iraqi Army, worked at Salman Pak for six months in the mid-1990s. Khodada defected to the United States in May 2001 and was interviewed by PBS's *Frontline* and the *New York Times* on October 14, 2001. He was encouraged to talk to the press by the Iraqi

National Congress, an Iraqi opposition group that had for more than a decade advocated the overthrow of Saddam Hussein. That he spoke so soon after the September 11 attacks and was prompted to do so by a group arguing for regime change in Iraq has led some to question Khodada's story.

At times, he came to conclusions not warranted by the evidence at that early date. The existence of an old airplane at the camp, for example, led Khodada to speculate that Iraq may have trained the September 11 hijackers. Throughout much of the *Frontline* interview, however, Khodada struck a moderate tone. When the interviewer asked him about chemical and biological weapons training at the camp, for instance, he admitted he had never seen any such instruction at Salman Pak, despite the fact that the camp was known by United Nations weapons inspectors throughout the early 1990s to house many of the Iraqi regime's biological weapons research facilities. And when Khodada was asked whether the "non-Iraqi Arabs" he observed at the camps were affiliated with Osama bin Laden, he responded that there was no way to know and that no one discussed such groups.

"This camp is specialized in exporting terrorism to the whole world," said Khodada, adding that it was run directly by the special operations division of Iraqi intelligence.

The sector of the camp devoted to training non-Iraqis was not visible from the surrounding roads, and its existence was concealed even from some high-ranking officials of Saddam's regime. Khodada described the instruction that took place in the camp. "Training is majorly on terrorism. They would be trained on assassinations, kidnapping, hijacking of airplanes, hijacking of buses, public buses, hijacking of trains and all other kinds of operations related to terrorism."

Saddam's fighters, such as the fedayeen, were also trained at the camp, but never together with foreigners.

They were special trainers or teachers from the Iraqi Intelligence and al-Mukhabarat. And those same trainers or teachers will train the fedayeen, the Iraqi fedayeen, and also the same group of those teachers will train the non-Iraqis, foreigners who are in the camp . . . The special training that I'm talking about, such as the kidnapping and so, is conducted by those trainers who are not from the army; they are from . . . al-Mukhabarat. And there was a person who is very famous. They call him Al-Shaba. This is an Arabic word that means "The Ghost," who was responsible for all the training, and those trainers or the teachers.

The Ghost, Khodada went on, is an Iraqi who "has conducted several terrorist operations in Lebanon and in other countries all over the world. And I know that he told us that he's been requested to be arrested by the Interpol. This is probably why he called himself the Ghost."

Even among employees at the camp, discussions of the terrorist instruction were discouraged. The Ghost "tried not to talk about training as much as possible," recalled Khodada. "I even, out of curiosity, asked him about those Arabs. Sometime he told me, 'Don't ask about them. This is something we're not supposed to talk about.' "

Khodada, who worked on administrative matters for the

camp, didn't observe the instruction firsthand. But he said it was known within the camp that it included a how-to course on suicide bombings. The training of foreign terrorists, he said, was much more rigorous than what the Iraqis at the camp received. "We know that Arabs, non-Iraqis who come to train in these kind of camps, are going to be sent to very dangerous and important operations outside Iraq; not inside Iraq. And they will be conducting very specific operations and dangerous operations in their own cities, or in their own countries, or other countries all over the world. Those Arabs are real volunteers. They come in small numbers, and they come with the intention to do some real suicidal operations."

The former Iraqi Army captain described, in vivid detail, the kinds of "self-confidence" training that fighters from the camp went through. They were told to jump from helicopters without knowing whether there was anything below them to soften their fall. In other exercises, trainees would "pull the pin of a hand grenade, and they will throw the hand grenade from one to another until the last one will throw it in the air and it will explode in the air," or "put a hand grenade in a pipe, and they will pull the pin and throw it in the pipe, and stand near the pipe saluting the hand grenade until it explodes. . . . And if you don't have self-confidence, you cannot do it."

There was little ambiguity about the purpose of such training, he said, which ranged from foreign language instruction to hijacking airplanes. "It has been said openly in the media and even to us, from the highest command, that the purpose of establishing Saddam's fighters is to attack American targets and American interests. This is known. There's no doubt about it. All this training is directed toward attacking American targets, and American interests."

Khodada said that Saddam reiterated those sentiments in a meeting with some of his soldiers on January 1, 1996. "We all met with Saddam personally," Khodada recalled. "And he told us we have to take revenge from America. Our duty is to attack and hit American targets in the Gulf, in the Arab world, and all over the world. He said that openly. When you volunteer to become Saddam's fighter . . . they will tell you the purpose of your volunteer[ing] is to attack American targets and American interests, not only in Iraq, not only in the Gulf, [but] all over the world, including Europe and America. That's how Saddam was able to attract those Arabs and Muslims who came to train, because that's exactly what they want to do."

UN inspectors independently verified the existence of the camps, and the airplane, at Salman Pak. When they asked the Iraqis for an explanation, they were told that the instruction focused not on terrorism but on counterterrorism. Satellite imagery taken by a private U.S. firm called Space Imaging on April 25, 2000, also confirmed the existence of an airplane, railroad cars, and a double-decker bus.

An Iraqi lieutenant general, also made available by the Iraqi National Congress, spoke to *Frontline* and the *New York Times* on November 6, 2001. He claimed to have observed training by Iraqi intelligence of small groups of non-Iraqi Arabs. "I was the security officer in charge of the unit. And through my responsibility for the security of the units and the camp itself, I've noticed that the Arab units remained there for a period of approximately five months before they left. And I saw a similar unit engaged in similar training during 2000."

The Iraqi commander said that the trainees were of various nationalities and were devoutly religious, interrupting their training several times a day to pray. The head trainer, he recalled, was named Jasem Rashid Zoubaa al Dolomi. "He was the special trainer for the Arabs, as they call them, because they were totally isolated and specialized."

The training was so secretive, he continued, it's possible even those closest to Saddam didn't know about it. "I'm sure that Saddam himself would know, but I'm not so sure about his sons that they would know. This is a closed camp which is under the direct control of the intelligence service itself. Because the special operations unit is under their control, Saddam Hussein himself."

Like those of Sabah Khodada, some of the lieutenant general's claims were extraordinary and speculative, such as his "gut feeling" that Iraqis were behind the September 11 attacks. But other statements were tempered: he refused, for example, to claim that the trainees were devotees of Osama bin Laden, saying that he had "no information of that kind."

The "non-Iraqi Arabs" trained at these facilities may not have been al Qaeda. None of the approximately 650 al Qaeda and Taliban detainees held in U.S. facilities at Guantanamo Bay, Cuba, has admitted training at Salman Pak. But there was no doubt about the activities at the camp.

According to Brigadier General Vincent Brooks, the spokesman for U.S. Central Command, coalition troops captured foreign fighters in the vicinity of the camp who spoke of having been trained there. At an April 6, 2003, press briefing, he said that Salman Pak was just one of "a number of examples we found where there's training activity happening inside of Iraq." Brooks specifically mentioned fighters from Sudan and Egypt, and said that information obtained from Iraqi detainees led him to believe "that there was terrorist training that was conducted at Salman Pak."

As Brooks indicated, the facility at Salman Pak was not the only terrorist training school in Iraq. In an interview before the war, Lieutenant General Riadh Abdallah, who left Iraq for the United States in 1999 and has never been affiliated with the Iraqi National Congress or any other exile groups, said that he was familiar with similar training at a facility north of Baghdad called Lake Tharthar. That camp, on the largest lake in Iraq, was known among Abdallah's Republican Guard colleagues as the "Salman Pak of the Sea."

Abdallah served on Saddam Hussein's personal security detail during the Gulf War, but fell out of favor with the former Iraqi dictator shortly after the war's end. His brother Abduli Alwhishah was a member of Saddam's rubber-stamp parliament from 1984 to 1991. Alwhishah had long opposed Saddam, but, like anyone who wanted to survive, he did so quietly. But after George H. W. Bush encouraged Shiites and Kurds to rise up following the Gulf War, Alwhishah joined the rebellion as a leader of its Nasiriya uprising. When Iraqi intelligence reported on Alwhishah's activities to headquarters in Baghdad, Abdallah was removed from his position in Saddam's Republican Guard, transferred to a job teaching new military recruits, and put on military probation. He was ordered to report weekly to Iraqi intelligence to ensure that he stayed in Iraq.

Abdallah considered himself lucky to have received such a

light punishment for his brother's defiance of the regime. Five of his fellow generals, including Barak Abdallah (no relation), a hero from the Iran-Iraq War, were executed for plotting against Saddam's government.

By 1993, after nearly two years in the Rafha refugee camp in Saudi Arabia, Alwhishah defected to the United States. Riadh Abdallah was promptly thrown in jail. "There was no judge. They just put you in."

Abdallah awoke thinking each day would be his last. "Every day they told me I would be executed," he says.

He was held in the same prison as Raji al Tikriti, Saddam's former doctor. Al Tikriti was suspected of trying to poison the former Iraqi dictator. His demise, says Abdallah, is "a very famous story in Iraq." Saddam's henchmen "made him food for dogs"—a crude execution Abdallah witnessed.

"They took us from jail and they put some blindfolds on our eyes and they took them off and we saw him. Before the dogs ate him we saw them read the judgment and they said why they were going to kill him. He was the head doctor for all the military, and he was the personal doctor for Saddam Hussein and for former Iraqi president Ahmed Hassan al Bakr."

The gruesome ceremony took place in a prison courtyard. Abdallah remembers that it was "wintertime," but cannot recall the exact date "because for eleven months I didn't see the sun, nothing—I didn't know what time." Abdallah later explained that Raji al Tikriti was dressed in "prison pajamas" with his hands and feet bound when this was done to him. Abdallah and seven other prisoners were forced to watch. The five dogs, he said, "were like big wolves." The doctor was alive when they were unleashed.

To Abdallah's surprise, after eleven months in prison, his captors released him and allowed him to return to teaching. He taught with other senior military officials who, he said, ran terrorist training operations at Salman Pak and Lake Tharthar. His fellow instructors spoke openly of their work at both locations. At Lake Tharthar, Abdallah says, terrorists were instructed in "diving, how to wire, how to put charges on ships, how to storm the ships, commando operations."

Was the camp for terrorists and the Iraqi military? "Terrorist. Not for the military. They were not Iraqi. They were all from other countries—maybe just a few Iraqis. And it's very confidential."

In 2003, three weeks before the Iraq War started, as anonymous intelligence officials and some in Congress scoffed at the Iraqi regime's support of international terror, Riadh Abdallah expressed bemused disbelief about the debate. "Saddam," he said, shaking his head, "is the father and the grandfather of terrorists."

CHAPTER SEVEN

CLINTON'S "CLOUD OF FEAR"

On November 15, 1997, with UN inspections once again faltering and tensions rising throughout the region, Saddam Hussein called for a campaign of terror. The newspaper *Babel*, the chief mouthpiece of the Iraqi regime—run by Uday Hussein, Saddam's eldest son—again urged Arabs to wage jihad against the West: "American and British interests, embassies, and naval ships in the Arab region should be the targets of military operations and commando attacks by Arab political forces." Iraqi television echoed these sentiments with a call to military units to prepare for another engagement in the "Mother of all Battles."

The flare-up in late 1997 was the latest in a seemingly endless series of disputes over UN weapons inspections. The language from both sides had become almost routine. Saddam threatened jihad. Bill Clinton promised to enforce the will of the international community. There was talk of diplomacy backed by force and tightened sanctions. No more cheat and retreat. An end to cat-and-mouse games. On it went.

But this time, the Clinton administration introduced another argument: chemical and biological weapons deployed by Saddam's henchmen or passed to terrorists who threatened Americans where they live. "Nothing concerned the Clinton Administration more than the dangers of WMD proliferation and the possibility of these terrible weapons falling into the hands of rogue states and terrorists," recalled Daniel Benjamin, a counterterrorism official on the National Security Council in the Clinton White House, in congressional testimony.

Clinton opened a speech in California on November 15, 1997, telling his audience that what they were about to hear was not meant to frighten them. But he proceeded to describe the gruesome aftermath of a chemical weapons attack two years earlier, pounding the lectern to emphasize his seriousness. Twelve people had died in a sarin gas attack in subways of Tokyo, and Americans, he argued, were not immune to such deadly attacks. World leaders must "do everything that can possibly be done not to let big stores of chemical and biological weapons fall into the wrong hands, not to let irresponsible people develop the capacity to put those big warheads on missiles or put them in briefcases that can be exploded in small rooms."

If the public rhetoric struck out in a new direction by emphasizing potential proliferation, the notion of Iraq sharing its weapons technology was not new. As far back as the Gulf War, rumors spread throughout intelligence and diplomatic circles that Iraq had shipped some of its deadly weapons and equipment to Libya, Sudan, and possibly even Iran. Those reports had been met with skepticism by Iraq specialists at the CIA, who reasoned that Saddam would be loath to part with his weapons, since his arsenal was precisely what allowed him to project his power throughout the region. After several years without confirmation, the rumors were largely dismissed.

But in 1995, the CIA began to see a stream of reporting that Iraq was helping Sudan establish a chemical weapons program. The agency had monitored Iraqi chemical weapons experts' travels to the African nation in 1995 and 1996, and the National Security Agency had intercepted phone calls from top Iraqi scientists to individuals associated with the Sudanese military that indicated collaboration on chemical weapons production. The fears that Clinton administration officials expressed in 1997 were based not on improbable hypotheticals, but on a growing pool of intelligence reports.

On November 16, 1997, the day after President Clinton's speech in California, his defense secretary, William Cohen, underscored the threat in an appearance on ABC's *This Week*. Cohen hoisted a five-pound bag of sugar onto the interview table and offered a grim scenario. "This amount of anthrax could be spread over a city—let's say the size of Washington. It would destroy at least half the population of that city," he warned ominously. Cohen held up a small vial of another substance. "VX is a nerve agent. One drop from this particular thimble as such—one single drop will kill you within a few minutes."

Although some critics accused the Clinton administration of overdramatizing the threats, a stunning article in the *Sunday Times of London* on that same day gave the public a bracing sense of the seriousness of Iraqi WMD proliferation. "Iraq is manufacturing poisonous gas at a secret location in Sudan," reported veteran journalist Jon Swain.

Bypassing the ban on weapons of mass destruction which the United Nations imposed on Baghdad after its defeat in the Gulf War, Saddam Hussein and the Islamist government of General Omar al Bashir in Khartoum are making and stockpiling mustard gas for their mutual benefit.

The *Sunday Times* has established through military intelligence and diplomatic sources in Kampala, the capital of neighbouring Uganda, that the gas is being made at a facility at Wau, in southwest Sudan, and that the Sudanese regime has already used it twice against rebels.

Production began in the autumn of 1995 under a clandestine deal between Khartoum and Baghdad to circumvent the UN's military and trade embargo on Iraq. The deal followed the visit of a high-level Iraqi military delegation, led by the head of the chemical weapons directorate of the Iraqi defence ministry.

The Sudanese opposition, which had claimed for some time that Bashir's government had used chemical weapons against their positions, identified ten sites suspected of manufacturing or storing chemical weapons. In a letter to Human Rights Watch, Mubarak al Madhi, the head of Sudan's National Democratic Alliance, an umbrella group of opposition parties, reported that an engineer and an intelligence official, both Iraqi Army colonels, worked with twelve Sudanese chemical engineers to develop chemical weapons. Although many of those claims were discounted as wartime propaganda, they were bolstered a short time later when the rebels found gas masks at a Sudanese government military installation.

On November 17, Clinton reiterated his concerns in im-promptu remarks at a Cessna plant in Wichita, Kansas. The chief concern, he told a crowd gathered for a speech on job training, was the prospect that deadly weapons could be passed to terrorists and other nonstate actors. "We must not allow the twenty-first century to go forward under a cloud of fear that terrorists, organized criminals, drug traffickers will terrorize people with chemical and biological weapons the way the nuclear threat hung over the heads of the whole world through the last half of this century."

Time magazine on newsstands the day of that speech re-ported on the threat. "Officials in Washington are deeply wor-ried about what some of them call 'strategic crime.' By that they mean the merging of the output from a government's ar-senals, like Saddam's biological weapons, with a group of semi-independent terrorists, like radical Islamist groups, who might slip such bioweapons into the United States and use them." Iraqi foreign minister Tariq Aziz, in an interview for the same article, denied that Iraq was involved in terrorism but raised the possibility that renewed attacks on Iraq could put "people in other countries" in the "mood" to conduct terror-ism in solidarity with Iraq.

Meanwhile, the Clinton administration continued to re-ceive reports from a variety of sources about collaboration be-tween Iraqi intelligence and radical Islamists. In a CNN appearance on November 17, Mohammed al Sabah, Kuwait's ambassador to the United States, said that "Saddam really has a proven track record of supporting terrorists all over the world. He still are [*sic*] very much engaging in this act."

The furious war of words between Iraq and the United States continued through the holidays and into the New Year. On February 10, 1998, excerpts from a draft of a memo from the House Task Force on Terrorism and Unconventional Warfare confirmed earlier press reports about collaboration between Iraq and Sudan. Publicly, the White House would neither confirm nor deny the charges. Defense Secretary Cohen, however, said that if the findings were accurate, they bolstered the tough White House stance on Iraq. In background discussions with reporters, senior Clinton administration officials dismissed the report as hype. It was a conclusion that would come back to haunt them.

The tensions peaked on February 17, 1998. President Clinton chose the Pentagon as the backdrop for a solemn address preparing the nation for war. The major television networks broke into their midday programming to carry the speech live. In a fierce, determined speech, Clinton warned of the "predators of the twenty-first century" and once again raised the possibility of the "reckless acts of outlaw nations and an unholy axis of terrorists, drug traffickers, and organized international criminals."

They will be all the more lethal if we allow them to build arsenals of nuclear, chemical and biological weapons and the missiles to deliver them. We simply cannot allow that to happen. There is no more clear example of this threat than Saddam Hussein's Iraq. His regime threatens the safety of his people, the stability of his region and the security of all the rest of us . . .

Now let's imagine the future. What if he fails to comply

and we fail to act, or we take some ambiguous third route which gives him yet more opportunities to develop this program of weapons of mass destruction and continue to press for the release of the sanctions and continue to ignore the solemn commitments that he made? Well, he will conclude that the international community has lost its will—its will. He will then conclude that he can go right on and do more to rebuild an arti—an arsenal of devastating destruction. And someday, some way, I guarantee you, he'll use the arsenal . . .

Saddam Hussein's Iraq reminds us of what we learned in the twentieth century and warns us of what we must know about the twenty-first. In this century, we learned through harsh experience that the only answer to aggression and illegal behavior is firmness, determination and, when necessary, action. In the next century, the community of nations may see more and more of the very kind of threat Iraq poses now—a rogue state with weapons of mass destruction, ready to use them or provide them to terrorists, drug traffickers or organized criminals who travel the world among us unnoticed.

But the Clinton administration did "take some ambiguous third route." UN Secretary General Kofi Annan negotiated yet another "last chance" deal in which the Iraqis agreed to allow inspectors to visit sensitive sites. This cooperation was predictably short-lived, and the inspectors left nine months later.

But President Clinton was prophetic in his warnings about cooperation between rogue states and terrorists. Two days after his speech, according to documents found in the bombed-out headquarters of Iraqi intelligence in April 2003, a senior official in Saddam's Mukhabarat circulated a three-page memo that would finalize plans for meetings in Baghdad between a representative of Osama bin Laden and Iraqi intelligence. The pages, each marked "Top Secret and Urgent," carried three separate dates: February 19, February 23, and February 24, 1998. The discovery, made by *Toronto Star* reporter Mitch Potter and Inigo Gilmore from the *Telegraph* in London and published on April 27, 2003, amounted "to the first hard evidence of contact between Osama bin Laden's al Qaeda organization and the Iraqi regime," according to Potter.

The memo said that Iraqi intelligence hoped "to gain the knowledge of the message from bin Laden and to convey to his envoy an oral message from us to bin Laden." The meetings in Baghdad would relate to "the future of our relationship with him [bin Laden], and to achieve a direct meeting with him." The meeting was not to be a get-together of low-level functionaries. According to the Iraqis, bin Laden would send "a trusted confidant."

The memo continued, "According to the above, we suggest permission to call the Khartoum station [Iraqi intelligence office in Sudan] to facilitate the travel arrangements for the above-mentioned person to Iraq. And that our body carry all the travel and hotel costs inside Iraq . . ."

The document was passed along to the deputy director of Iraqi intelligence, with a recommendation that "the deputy director general bring the envoy to Iraq because we may find in this envoy a way to maintain contacts with bin Laden." Handwritten notes on the third page of the memo indicate that the envoy arrived on March 5, 1998, and stayed as a guest of the

Iraqi regime at Baghdad's Mansur Melia Hotel. Additional margin notes suggest that the meetings were extended by a week—for a total of sixteen days.

Aside from the obvious bombshell—confirmation of another, previously unknown meeting between high-level Iraqi intelligence and a senior al Qaeda official—the most striking aspect of the memo is the light it sheds on the great lengths to which Iraqi intelligence went to keep the relationship secret.

Despite the fact that the memo was an internal document, each of the three references to "bin Laden" had been covered by correction fluid. Even among Saddam's most trusted Mukhabarat henchmen, the relationship between Iraq and al Qaeda was shrouded in secrecy. Iraqi intelligence officials were referred to in code, never by their names. One of the pages was sent by "MD1/3" to "M4/7." According to Potter, notes in the margin are signed, once again in code, by the deputy director of Iraqi intelligence. The memo also warns against communicating in writing.

The discovery of the memo was also valuable for what it reveals about American intelligence and the media. Given the intensity of the prewar debate about Iraq's links with al Qaeda, one would think that the discovery of a document directly linking al Qaeda and Iraqi intelligence and discussing their "future relationship" would be big news. But Americans who relied on the *New York Times* never read about the document. The same was true for readers of the *Washington Post*. (In those early postwar days, the American media was obsessed with reports of the looting of Iraq's antiquities, almost all of which turned out to be false.)

CBS Radio's Charles Osgood interviewed Potter and

Gilmore, who explained how they found the file and had it translated back in their hotel room. (The document was eventually translated by five separate Arabic-speaking translators for accuracy.) Osgood summed up the report this way: "U.S. officials would be interested in reviewing the documents, but until they do, the link is regarded as an uncorroborated press report."

Incredibly, Osgood was wrong. U.S. officials were apparently not interested in reviewing the documents showing a direct link between al Qaeda and Iraqi intelligence. The reporters who obtained the memo had, nearly a year after finding it, not been contacted by the CIA or anyone else from the U.S. government.

This oversight is at the very least odd. February 1998 appears to have been a particularly active month in the relationship. The CIA has reporting from a "regular and reliable source" about meetings between al Qaeda and Iraqi intelligence earlier in February, at the height of harsh rhetorical exchanges between Saddam and the United States. The intelligence summarized in the Feith memo includes information that bin Laden's top deputy, Ayman al Zawahiri, "visited Baghdad and met with the Iraqi Vice President on 3 February 1998. The goal of the visit was to arrange for coordination between Iraq and bin Laden and establish camps in al-Falluja, an-Nasiriya, and Iraqi Kurdistan under the leadership of Abdul Aziz."

The visit coincided with a payment of $300,000 from Iraqi intelligence to Zawahiri's Egyptian Islamic Jihad, which merged that same year with al Qaeda. The funding, first reported in *U.S. News & World Report*, was disclosed to U.S. officials by a "senior member" of Iraqi intelligence. Although the report came from a single source, an administration official later confirmed it, calling it "a lock." The payment, this source says, went directly to Zawahiri.

Six days after President Clinton spoke to the nation about the possibility of war with Iraq, Zawahiri and bin Laden issued their now-famous fatwa instructing followers to kill Americans—military and civilians. The message, which came from a new group called the "World Islamic Front for Jihad Against the Jews and Crusaders," made three separate references to Iraq, citing U.S. policy there as the "best proof" of America's aggressive intentions in the Middle East.

> First, for over seven years the United States has been occupying the lands of Islam in the holiest of places, the Arabian Peninsula, plundering its riches, dictating to its rulers, humiliating its people, terrorizing its neighbors, and turning its bases in the Peninsula into a spearhead through which to fight the neighboring Muslim peoples. . . . The best proof of this is the Americans' continuing aggression against the Iraqi people using the Peninsula as a staging post, even though all its rulers are against their territories being used to that end, still they are helpless. Second, despite the great devastation inflicted on the Iraqi people by the crusader-Zionist alliance, and despite the huge number of those killed, in excess of 1 million . . . despite all this, the Americans are once again trying to repeat the horrific massacres, as though they are not content with the protracted blockade imposed after the ferocious war or the fragmentation and devastation.

The Americans, bin Laden said, are working on behalf of Israel. "The best proof of this is their eagerness to destroy Iraq, the strongest neighboring Arab state, and their endeavor to fragment all the states of the region such as Iraq, Saudi Arabia, Egypt, and Sudan into paper statelets and through their disunion and weakness to guarantee Israel's survival and the continuation of the brutal crusade occupation of the Peninsula."

Bin Laden urged his followers to act. "The ruling to kill all Americans and their allies—civilians and military—is an individual duty for every Muslim who can do it in any country in which it is possible to do it."

The U.S. intelligence community, meanwhile, continued to track the relationship between Iraq and Sudan. Evidence of collaboration on chemical weapons mounted. In the spring of 1998, the CIA dispatched an operative to obtain a soil sample from a facility outside the Sudanese capital of Khartoum suspected of producing precursor chemicals for the deadly nerve gas VX. The sample showed high levels of one chemical used to produce the gas, O-ethylmethylphosphonothioic acid, known as EMPTA.

The CIA also stepped up efforts to capture bin Laden. Working with a group of Afghan fighters, the agency's al Qaeda unit drafted several different plans to capture bin Laden as he traveled from cave to training camp, from big cities to Afghanistan's rural mountains. The plans, derided as far-fetched by some terrorism specialists at the White House and the National Security Council, were never set in motion.

On August 7, 1998, al Qaeda made good on bin Laden's threats to kill Americans. Bombers struck almost simultaneously at the U.S. embassies in Kenya and Tanzania, killing 257 people—including 12 Americans—and wounding nearly 5,000.

The Clinton administration determined within five days that al Qaeda was responsible for the attacks and moved swiftly to retaliate. One of the targets would be in Afghanistan. But the Clinton national security team wanted to strike simultaneously at two targets, much as the terrorists had. "The decision to go to [Sudan] was an add-on," says a senior intelligence official involved in the decision. "They wanted a dual strike." A small group of Clinton administration officials, led by CIA director George Tenet and national security adviser Sandy Berger, reviewed a number of al Qaeda-linked targets in the Sudan. Although bin Laden had left the Sudan two years earlier, U.S. officials believed that he was still deeply involved in the Sudanese government–run Military Industrial Corporation (MIC).

The Clinton team reviewed the intelligence on several weapons-related sites in the Sudan, most of them in or around Khartoum. Berger and his deputies were very concerned about collateral damage and excluded several potential targets because of their proximity to residential neighborhoods. On August 17, 1998, CIA director Tenet presented the White House with evidence that the al Shifa pharmaceutical plant on the outskirts of Khartoum was involved in the production of VX nerve gas.

On August 20, 1998, sixty-six Tomahawk missiles slammed into an al Qaeda training camp in Afghanistan, and another thirteen hit the al Shifa plant. The Afghanistan strike was thought to have targeted a terrorist summit scheduled for that day. But the gathering had been postponed, and top al Qaeda leaders had left the camp days earlier.

President Clinton explained the strikes in an Oval Office address to the nation. In addition to the camps in Afghanistan, Clinton said U.S. forces "attacked a factory in Sudan associated with the bin Laden network. The factory was involved in the production of materials for chemical weapons." In a press briefing the following day, Sandy Berger was more emphatic. "Let me be very clear about this. There is no question in my mind that the Sudanese factory was producing chemicals that are used—can be used—in VX gas. This was a plant that was producing chemical warfare–related weapons and we have physical evidence of that fact."

Almost immediately, the decision to strike at al Shifa aroused controversy. Sudanese foreign minister Osman Ismail, who had arrived in Baghdad the day of the attack for what was described as a previously scheduled meeting with Saddam Hussein, denied that the plant had any involvement in chemical weapons production and invited the United Nations to send inspectors to the site. Although U.S. officials had expressed skepticism that the plant produced pharmaceuticals, reporters on the ground in Sudan found aspirin bottles and a variety of other indications that the plant did, in fact, manufacture drugs.

To demonstrate that the plant was operating according to international law, Ismail pointed out that the al Shifa plant had won a contract for $199,000 to provide medicine to Iraq through a United Nations program. But the contract raised suspicions among U.S. intelligence officials, principally because there was no record of the goods having been delivered to Iraq in the eight months between when the contract was signed and the United States bombed the plant.

Hours after the attack, Iraq's Revolutionary Command Council issued a statement on Iraqi television condemning the attacks, and called for Arabs to "reeducate" America about its policies in the region. The Iraqi regime accused the United States of "systematic international terrorism" and vowed to help "any Arab and international countries to confront the U.S. hostile policies." Other Arab countries also condemned the attacks.

With journalists and the international community demanding more details on the targeting of al Shifa, the Clinton administration relented. On August 24, 1998, the administration made available a "senior intelligence official" for a background briefing with reporters. The briefer cited "strong ties between the plant and Iraq" as one of the justifications for attacking it. Although this official was careful not to oversell bin Laden's ties to the plant, other members of Clinton's national security team told reporters that the plant's general manager lived in a villa owned by bin Laden.

The next day, Thomas Pickering, undersecretary of state for political affairs and one of a handful of Clinton officials involved in the decision to strike al Shifa, briefed foreign reporters at the National Press Club.

> With respect to Sudan, I think that it is important to know and understand that we have been aware for at least two years that there was a serious potential problem at this plant that was struck, that we had related important physical evidence which was acquired by the United States in recent months. The physical evidence is a soil sample. Analysis of it shows the presence of a chemical whose simple name is

EMPTA, a known precursor for the nerve agent VX, and an indicator of a potential to produce VX gas. The substance is not used in commercial applications. It doesn't occur naturally in the environment, and it is not a by-product of another chemical process.

Pickering was asked directly whether he knew "of any connection between the so-called pharmaceutical plant in Khartoum and the Iraqi government in regard to production of precursors of VX." He answered carefully: "Yeah, I would like to consult my notes just to be sure that what I have to say is stated clearly and correctly. We see evidence that we think is quite clear on contacts between Sudan and Iraq. In fact, El Shifa officials, early in the company's history, we believe were in touch with Iraqi individuals associated with Iraq's VX program."

John McWethy, national security correspondent for ABC News, described the connection this way on the August 25, 1998, edition of *World News Tonight* with Peter Jennings: "The U.S. had been suspicious for months, partly because of Osama bin Laden's financial ties, but also because of strong connections to Iraq. Sources say the U.S. had intercepted phone calls from the plant to a man in Iraq who runs that country's chemical weapons program."

Bill Richardson, at the time U.S. ambassador to the United Nations, echoed those sentiments in an appearance on CNN's *Late Edition with Wolf Blitzer* on August 30, 1998. He called the targeting "one of the finest hours of our intelligence people." Richardson said, "We know for a fact [there was] physical evidence, soil samples of VX precursor—[a] chemical precursor—at the site." He cited "direct evidence of ties between Osama bin Laden" and Sudan's Military Industrial Corporation. "You combine that with Sudan support for terrorism, their connections with Iraq on VX, and you combine that, also, with the chemical precursor issue, and Sudan's leadership support for Osama bin Laden, and you've got a pretty clear-cut case."

For journalists and many at the CIA, however, the case was hardly clear-cut. For one thing, U.S. intelligence had collected the soil sample from outside the plant's front gate, not within the grounds, despite the fact that an internal CIA memo issued a month before the attacks had recommended gathering additional soil samples from the site before reaching conclusions. "It caused a lot of heartburn at the agency," recalls a former top intelligence official.

Not surprisingly, Iraq denied any involvement. The political editor of Radio Iraq read a statement on the air, saying that "the Clinton government has fabricated yet another lie to the effect that Iraq had helped Sudan produce this chemical weapon. The U.S. government knows very well that neither Sudan nor Iraq can or actually seeks to produce such a weapon."

Even as Iraq denied helping Sudan and al Qaeda with weapons of mass destruction, the regime lauded Osama bin Laden. On August 27, 1998, twenty days after al Qaeda attacked the U.S. embassies in Africa, *Babel,* Uday Hussein's newspaper, published a startling editorial proclaiming bin Laden "an Arab and Islamic hero."

With the Clinton administration defending its decision to strike in Sudan by citing Iraqi ties to the plant, bin Laden's connections with the plant also came under intense scrutiny. Salah Idris, a wealthy businessman, had purchased the factory five months before the attacks. The Treasury Department froze his assets after the attacks, but neglected to pursue the case when Idris sued the U.S. government for the release of his money. U.S. officials had "concerns" about Idris, but dropped the case rather than expose sensitive "sources and methods" in court. Idris was later found to have a close relationship with Sheikh Khalid bin Mahfouz, a chief bin Laden financier, but these ties were not known before the strikes on al Shifa.

And some intelligence officials continued to back the targeting even after the public controversy. John C. Gannon, then chairman of the National Intelligence Council, defended the strikes in a speech at Stanford University on November 16, 1998.

We found solid evidence of CW [chemical weapons] activity at Shifa in Khartoum. Sophisticated tests done on soil samples revealed the presence of EMPTA, a key precursor for the nerve agent VX. Perhaps if our information had been derived by less technical means, means more readily understood by the public, the case would not have been received with such skepticism. But, I emphasize, the evidence was solid. Moreover, the evidence fit into the ominous pattern we had been piecing together against bin Laden and his network. Bin Laden had attacked Americans before and he said he planned to do so again. He was seeking CW to use in future attacks. He was cooperating with the government of Sudan in those efforts. Shifa was linked to bin Laden and CW. We brought the evidence and our analyses to the President, and he took decisive action.

Independent experts also found a connection between bin Laden and the Sudanese chemical weapons programs. *Jane's Intelligence Review*, a respected military and intelligence journal, published a report, shortly before the U.S. attacks, based on minutes of an October 1996 meeting of Sudanese officials who claimed that bin Laden had agreed to finance a chemical weapons facility in Kubar, a suburb of Khartoum.

Still, in interviews and public appearances, several high-level members of Clinton's national security team defended the decision to strike al Shifa. Daniel Benjamin, who worked on the NSC counterterrorism staff, says, "The bottom line for me is that the targeting was justified and appropriate . . . I would be surprised if any president—with the evidence of al Qaeda's intentions evident in Nairobi and Dar es Salaam and the intelligence on [chemical weapons] that was at hand from Sudan—would have made a different decision about bombing the plant." Another top official, who spoke on the condition of anonymity, was equally emphatic: "The intelligence was solid."

On March 23, 2004, former defense secretary Cohen offered a vigorous defense of the targeting before the commission investigating the September 11 attacks. He noted that the intelligence reporting indicated that the al Shifa plant had been constructed under tight security and that an executive from the plant "traveled to Baghdad to meet with the father of the VX program." He responded to criticism that the intelligence was not good enough to justify an attack by asking the commissioners to envision a similar hearing conducted in the aftermath of a chemical weapons attack.

I put myself in the position of coming before you and having someone like you say to me, "Let me get this straight, Mr. Secretary, we've just had a chemical weapons attack upon our cities or our troops and we've lost several hundred or several thousand. And this is the information which you had at your fingertips. You had a plant that was built under the following circumstances, you had a manager that went to Baghdad, you had Osama bin Laden who had funded at least the corporation, and you had traces of EMPTA and you did what? You did nothing? Is that a responsible activity on the part of the Secretary of Defense?"

And the answer is pretty clear. So I was satisfied, even though that still is pointed as a mistake, that it was the right thing to do then. I would do it again, based on that kind of intelligence.

Several Bush administration policy makers believe their predecessors got it right. "There's pretty good intelligence linking al Shifa with Iraq and also good information linking al Shifa to al Qaeda," says one administration official familiar with the intelligence. "I don't think there's much dispute that MIC [Sudan's Military Industrial Corporation] was al Qaeda supported. The link from al Shifa to Iraq is what there's more dispute about."

On August 31, 1998, Iraqi vice president Taha Yasin Ramadan left for a trip to Sudan. Ramadan, in a statement to the Iraqi News Agency, "said that his visit to Sudan comes within the framework of consultation and dialogue over the development of cooperation and coordination between the two fraternal countries in order to face up to the U.S. and Zionist schemes and acts of aggression against the Arab nation."

U.S. intelligence officials believe that Sudanese leaders, acting on bin Laden's behalf, asked Ramadan if Iraq would give bin Laden asylum. The offer was first reported by Sheila MacVicar of ABC News on January 14, 1999. "Three weeks after the bombing, on August 31, bin Laden reaches out to his friends in Iraq and Sudan. Iraq's vice president arrives in Khartoum to show his support for the Sudanese after the U.S. attack . . . during these meetings, senior Sudanese officials acting on behalf of bin Laden ask if Saddam Hussein would grant him asylum."

Al Qaeda's collaboration with Iraq on weapons of mass destruction was noted in a Clinton administration indictment of bin Laden written in the spring of 1998, before the embassy bombings. The Clinton Justice Department had been concerned about a negative public reaction to capturing bin Laden without official paperwork charging him with a crime and needed a vehicle for his extradition. Including the al Qaeda–Iraq connection in the indictment was "not an afterthought," says an official familiar with the deliberations. "It couldn't have gotten into the indictment unless someone was willing to testify to it under oath." The Clinton administration's indictment was unequivocal:

Al Qaeda reached an understanding with the government of Iraq that al Qaeda would not work against that government and that on particular projects, specifically including weapons development, al Qaeda would work cooperatively with the Government of Iraq.

From the various reports on the Iraq–Sudan–bin Laden–al Shifa connection, a consensus emerged: both Iraq and bin Laden worked with the Sudanese Military Industrial Corporation to produce chemical weapons. The question, to some, was whether Iraq knew that bin Laden was on the receiving end of its technology and, conversely, whether bin Laden knew that Iraq was its supplier.

"The Iraqi connection with al Shifa, given what we know about it, does not yet meet the test as proof of a substantive relationship because it isn't clear that one side knew the other side's involvement," says Daniel Benjamin, the former Clinton administration counterterrorism official.

That is, it is not clear that the Iraqis knew about bin Laden's well-concealed investment in the Sudanese Military Industrial Corporation. The Sudanese very likely had their own interest in VX development, and they would also have had good reasons to keep al Qaeda's involvement from the Iraqis. After all, Saddam was exactly the kind of secularist autocrat that al Qaeda despised. In the most extreme case, if the Iraqis suspected al Qaeda involvement, they might have had assurances from the Sudanese that bin Laden's people would never get the weapons. That may sound less than satisfying, but the Sudanese did show a talent for fleecing bin Laden. It is all somewhat speculative, and it would be helpful to know more.

That view was seconded by Winston Wiley, former deputy CIA director. Asked whether it would be possible for both sides to be so clueless, given the close relationship between Sudanese intelligence and al Qaeda, he said, "It's not surprising at all. It may be that the Sudanese thought the Mother of All Secularists is giving me this stuff and the Mother of All Fundamentalists is getting it. There is a premium of confidentiality for its own sake. I think the burden of proof is to demonstrate that they did know about each other, rather than assuming that simply because these lines intersected that they must have known."

But others disagree. "It was common knowledge that he [bin Laden] was commingled with the Sudanese government," says Stanley Bedlington, the former senior analyst in the CIA's counterterrorism center. "The fact that the Iraqis didn't know this seems unlikely."

The fact remains that six senior Clinton administration national security officials are on the record defending the al Shifa strikes, citing an Iraqi connection. Those strikes, of course, came in response to attacks conducted by al Qaeda. Whether Iraq and al Qaeda were knowingly working together is an interesting but secondary concern for Bush administration policy makers. That Iraq was providing technology and knowhow to bin Laden—even if indirectly and unwittingly—demonstrated the danger of leaving Saddam in place.

And by the time President Bush had to decide on war with Iraq, the picture of potential Iraq–al Qaeda collaboration on WMD had become much clearer.

CHAPTER EIGHT

THE CONNECTION MAKES THE PAPERS

Ibn al Sheikh al Libi was one of the first high-ranking al Qaeda terrorists detained after September 11. A member of bin Laden's inner circle, he was responsible for years for the Khalden training camp outside Kandahar, Afghanistan, which trained many of the perpetrators of the 1993 World Trade Center bombing, the 1998 Africa embassy bombings, and the September 11 attacks. Among its alumni are terrorists who have in recent days become household names, including Mohamed Atta, Zacarias Moussaoui, and "shoe bomber" Richard Reid.

Al Libi was captured by Pakistani forces in November 2001, and unlike many other al Qaeda leaders in captivity, he soon began talking openly to his interrogators. For months, al Libi provided the U.S. government solid, "actionable" intelligence on al Qaeda operations. He also spoke openly about collaboration between al Qaeda and Iraq on weapons of mass destruction. In an early debriefing, al Libi said he became involved in the direct discussions between Iraqi intelligence and al Qaeda about cooperation on WMD in 1996, later revising the date to 1997.

CIA director George Tenet presented al Libi's reporting to the Senate Intelligence Committee in the fall of 2002. "We have credible reporting that al Qaeda leaders sought contacts in Iraq who could help them acquire WMD capabilities," said an unclassified summary of the testimony. "The reporting also stated that Iraq has provided training to al Qaeda members in the areas of poisons and gases and making conventional bombs."

Colin Powell, too, gave an overview of al Libi's reporting in his February 5, 2003, presentation to the United Nations Security Council.

This senior al Qaeda terrorist was responsible for one of al Qaeda's training camps in Afghanistan. His information comes firsthand from his personal involvement at senior levels of al Qaeda. He says bin Laden and his top deputy in Afghanistan, deceased al Qaeda leader Mohammed Atef, did not believe that al Qaeda labs in Afghanistan were capable enough to manufacture these chemical or biological agents. They needed to go somewhere else; they had to look outside of Afghanistan for help. Where did they go, where did they look? They went to Iraq.

The support that he describes included Iraq offering chemical or biological weapons training for two al Qaeda associates, beginning in December 2000. He says that a militant known as Abu Abdullah al-Iraqi had been sent to Iraq several times between 1997 and 2000 for help in acquiring poisons and gases. Abdullah al-Iraqi characterized the relationship he forged with Iraqi officials as "successful." As I said at the outset, none of this should come as a surprise to any of us. Terrorism has been a tool used by Saddam for decades. Saddam was a supporter of terrorism long before these terrorist networks had a name and this support continues. The nexus of poisons and terror is new. The nexus of Iraq and terror is old. The combination is lethal.

Al Qaeda had, of course, been working for years to develop WMD in Sudan and Afghanistan. "I know the [WMD] camps existed," recalls a former top CIA official. "I know there were chemicals. We had on satellite imagery very clear photos. We had pictures of dead dogs and other animals outside of bin Laden's camp in Afghanistan. We called them 'laboratories,' but we didn't know whether they were doing research or building weapons. We didn't know."

Whatever advances al Qaeda made, it wasn't enough for bin Laden, who became increasingly frustrated. "Each time they made some progress they would blow up a lab or otherwise have a setback," says one Bush administration official. So at bin Laden's request, al Libi and Mohammed Atef recruited Abu Abdullah al Iraqi to travel to Baghdad and ask Iraqi intelligence for assistance. When he returned, he reported that the Iraqis were open to providing help, but insisted on keeping the relationship secret. Al Libi later told the CIA that bin Laden was encouraged and was especially pleased that the Iraqis shared his desire for secrecy; subsequent CIA analysis suggests that bin Laden wanted to keep the relationship quiet for fear of dissent within his ranks.

Abu Abdullah al Iraqi made a second trip to meet with the Iraqi intelligence service and came back with specific instructions: recruit two "non-Arab, English-speaking" liaisons. A U.S. official familiar with the intelligence speculates that by recruiting an emissary who didn't fit the profile of an al Qaeda terrorist or an Iraqi intelligence officer, Saddam might be better positioned to deny the arrangement were its particulars revealed. Al Libi obliged. He recruited one Filipino and another go-between of unknown nationality, both of whom spoke English fluently.

Abu Abdullah al Iraqi took his new recruits to introduce them to his Iraqi Intelligence Service contacts. Al Libi remembers that this third trip took place shortly after the bombing of the USS *Cole* on October 12, 2000. A summary of al Libi's debriefing in the Feith memo reports that "two al Qaeda operatives were sent to Iraq for CBW [chemical/biological weapons] related training beginning in Dec 2000." Iraqi intelligence, he said, had been "encouraged" by the successful embassy and USS *Cole* bombings, and the training was approved.

Al Libi's description of the Iraqi reaction to deadly terrorist attacks corroborates several other reports that Saddam increased support for radical groups after they demonstrated their lethality. A senior Iraqi intelligence officer interrogated by a foreign government service whose debriefing was summarized in the Feith memo indicated that "Iraq increased support to Palestinian groups after major terrorist attacks and that the change in Iraqi relations with al Qaeda after the embassy bombings followed this pattern." A leader of the al Qaeda–linked Abu Sayyaf group in the Philippines who said that his group received Iraqi money also noted that the funding spiked after successful attacks.

These were hardly the only contacts between Iraqi intelligence and al Qaeda during this time. Following the meeting between Ayman al Zawahiri and senior Iraqi officials on February 3, 1998, and the subsequent sixteen-day visit to Baghdad by a bin Laden confidant in March, a small band of al Qaeda leaders traveled to Iraq in April to celebrate Saddam's sixty-first birthday.

Iraqi media devoted a full day of programming to praising their leader, and influential Baath Party members reportedly handed out pastries and presents to Iraqi citizens. Meanwhile, the al Qaeda visitors accompanied their hosts, Uday and Qusay Hussein, Saddam's sons, to an extravagant celebration in Tikrit. Postwar intelligence reporting from a variety of sources indicates that Qusay Hussein, Saddam's younger and more trusted son, became a primary contact with al Qaeda.

According to CIA reporting summarized in the Feith memo, a foreign government service interrogated a senior Iraqi intelligence officer who defected in late 1998. This source "had direct access to the information," and corroborated previous reporting that the relationship intensified after the 1998 embassy bombings and that "the Iraqi intelligence service station in Pakistan was Baghdad's main point of contact with al Qaeda."

On December 16, 1998, after yet another impasse on UN weapons inspections, President Clinton ordered a seventy-hour bombing raid in Iraq. According to intelligence reporting summarized in the Feith memo, the contacts between Iraq and al Qaeda increased.

A "foreign government service reported that an Iraqi delegation, including at least two Iraqi Intelligence officers formerly assigned to the Iraqi Embassy in Pakistan, met in late

1998 with bin Laden in Afghanistan." A CIA report contains virtually identical information, and also notes that Zawahiri was present at the meeting.

And more:

> Iraq sent an Iraqi intelligence officer to Afghanistan to seek closer ties to bin Laden and the Taliban in late 1998. The source reported that the Iraqi regime was trying to broaden its cooperation with al Qaeda. Iraq was looking to recruit "Muslim elements" to sabotage U.S. and UK interests. After a senior Iraqi intelligence officer met with Taliban leader Omar, arrangements were made for a series of meetings between the Iraqi intelligence officer and bin Laden in Pakistan. The source noted Faruq Hijazi was in Afghanistan in late 1998.

Hijazi traveled to Afghanistan again. "According to foreign government service sensitive CIA reporting, Faruq Hijazi went to Afghanistan in 1999 along with several other Iraqi officials to meet with bin Laden. The source claimed that Hijazi would have met bin Laden only at Saddam's explicit direction."

A Pentagon analysis included after this report notes that the intelligence on meetings between Iraqi intelligence and al Qaeda in Afghanistan and Pakistan during the late 1990s comes from six different sources that corroborate one another.

For much of the relationship, the contacts were known only to a small cadre of intelligence officials. That all ended late in 1998. The connection was widely reported in the American and international media, and the unlikely relationship between Iraq and al Qaeda almost overnight seemed not so unlikely. Pundits, former intelligence officers, and unnamed government officials speculated about the relationship and its dangerous implications for the world. The information in the news reports came from foreign and domestic intelligence services. And it was featured in mainstream publications—regional newspapers, international wire services, prominent newsweeklies, network radio and television broadcasts.

The same information previously hidden away in secret files of intelligence agencies, with titles like "CIA TD 314/32264-01," was suddenly available to the rest of the world, in articles with headlines like "Saddam + Bin Laden?" which ran over a story in *Newsweek*'s January 11, 1999, issue that said, "Here's what is known so far: Saddam Hussein, who has a long record of supporting terrorism, is trying to rebuild his intelligence network overseas—assets that would allow him to establish a terrorism network. U.S. sources say he is reaching out to Islamic terrorists, including some who may be linked to Osama bin Laden, the wealthy Saudi exile accused of masterminding the bombing of two U.S. embassies in Africa last summer."

In the story, an "Arab intelligence source who knows Saddam personally and stays in touch with his clandestine service" predicted that "very soon you will be seeing large-scale terrorist activity run by the Iraqis." *Newsweek* noted that officials in Washington were "skeptical," but added that the Arab source said operations were under way with Saddam outsourcing terror—using "false flags" to give him deniability after attacks. Palestinians, Iranians, and al Qaeda, the Arab source said, all "have representatives in Baghdad."

Some Washington officials were dubious, but others were

not. On January 14, 1999, ABC News reported that three intelligence agencies believed that Saddam had offered asylum to bin Laden.

> Intelligence sources say bin Laden's long relationship with the Iraqis began as he helped Sudan's fundamentalist government in their efforts to acquire weapons of mass destruction. . . . ABC News has learned that in December, an Iraqi intelligence chief, named Faruq Hijazi, now Iraq's ambassador to Turkey, made a secret trip to Afghanistan to meet with bin Laden. Three intelligence agencies tell ABC News they cannot be certain what was discussed, but almost certainly, they say, bin Laden has been told he would be welcome in Baghdad.

NPR reporter Mike Shuster turned to Vincent Cannistraro, former head of the CIA's counterterrorism center.

CANNISTRARO: Faruq Hijazi, who was the Iraqi ambassador in Turkey, went to Afghanistan in December with the knowledge of the Taliban and met with Osama bin Laden. It's known through a variety of intelligence reports that the U.S. has, but it's also known through sources in Afghanistan, members of Osama's entourage let it be known that the meeting had taken place.

SHUSTER: Iraq's contacts with bin Laden go back some years, to at least 1994, when, according to one U.S. government source, Hijazi met him when bin Laden lived in Sudan. According to Cannistraro, Iraq invited bin

Laden to live in Baghdad to be nearer to potential targets of terrorist attack in Saudi Arabia and Kuwait . . . some experts believe bin Laden might be tempted to live in Iraq because of his reported desire to obtain chemical or biological weapons. CIA director George Tenet referred to that in recent testimony before the Senate Armed Services Committee when he said bin Laden was planning additional attacks on American targets.

There is precedent for Saddam accommodating terrorists. He had welcomed Abu Abbas, mastermind of the hijacking of the *Achille Lauro* cruise ship in 1985. (Abbas was captured by U.S. troops in Baghdad on April 14, 2003, and later died in U.S. custody.)

And at the same time Saddam was reported to have offered asylum to bin Laden, he received another high-profile terrorist, Sabri al Banna, in Baghdad. Throughout the 1970s and 1980s, Al Banna, better known as Abu Nidal, ranked among the world's most wanted terrorists. A representative from the Lebanon office of the Abu Nidal Organization told the Associated Press that al Banna went to Baghdad "with the full knowledge and preparations of the Iraqi authorities."

As the world speculated about bin Laden's next move, the United States began to pressure the Taliban government in Afghanistan to sever all ties with him. Mullah Omar, the Taliban leader, was in a difficult spot. Defying the United States risked a war his ragtag troops were sure to lose. But bin Laden had been as good to the Taliban as he had been to the government of Sudan, supplying the destitute Afghanistan with money and arms in exchange for safe haven. The relationship was based as much on state sponsorship of a terrorist group as it was on a terrorist group sponsoring a state.

In mid-February 1998, the Taliban announced that the al Qaeda leader had gone "missing" from Afghanistan. The report was met with skepticism, and in July, the Taliban finally acknowledged that bin Laden was still there.

According to Khalil Ibrahim Abdallah, a former assistant for operations in the Iraqi Intelligence Service captured by coalition forces in April 2003, bin Laden requested a meeting with Saddam in July 1999. A summary of Abdallah's debriefing reads: "The guidance sent back from Saddam's office reportedly ordered Iraqi intelligence to refrain from any further contact with bin Laden and al Qaeda. The source opined that Saddam wanted to distance himself from al Qaeda" and said that the message was "the last contact" between Iraq and al Qaeda.

The bulk of intelligence reporting on the relationship, though, contradicts his claim that the relationship ended in the summer of 1999. It may be that Abdallah wasn't privy to further communications, but that doesn't mean they didn't take place.

That aside, Abdallah's words are interesting for another reason: he is the latest in a long line of senior Iraqi intelligence officials and al Qaeda detainees with knowledge of the relationship. And it might go without saying that there would be no need for Saddam to "distance himself" from bin Laden if they hadn't had relations in the past.

In any case, several months after Saddam had allegedly decided to cut ties with bin Laden, he strongly reconsidered. If, as U.S. intelligence officials believe, Hijazi had offered bin Laden asylum, the al Qaeda leader didn't immediately act on the invitation. According to a report from the National Security Agency, the Iraqis considered extending their generous offer again: "An NSA report said that Iraqi officials were carefully considering offering safe haven to bin Laden and his closest collaborators in Nov 1999. The source indicated the idea was put forward by the presumed head of Iraqi intelligence in Islamabad (Khalid Janaby) who in turn was in frequent contact and had good relations with bin Laden."

The contacts continued. According to a Pentagon analysis of CIA intelligence reporting, various sources reported in 1999, as in years past, "that the springboard for contacts between Iraq and al Qaeda was the Iraqi Embassy in Pakistan."

Throughout late 1998 and early 1999, media reports about the Iraq–al Qaeda relationship were common. That the two were in league was quickly becoming accepted wisdom, so much so that reporters didn't feel the need to source claims of cooperation and asylum offers. By February 14, 1999, the *Washington Post* ran an AP story that ended this way: "The Iraqi President Saddam Hussein has offered asylum to bin Laden, who openly supports Iraq against Western powers."

The attention to the connection would be short-lived.

CHAPTER NINE

WHAT HAPPENED IN PRAGUE?

For nearly a year after the September 11 attacks, the most disputed of the Iraq–al Qaeda connections was the one between lead hijacker Mohamed Atta and Iraqi intelligence. Early news reports suggested that Atta had met a high-ranking intelligence officer in Prague, Czech Republic, just six months before the attacks. If true, the encounter would have presented a direct and ominous connection between those attacks and the government of Iraq.

Reports of the meeting appeared just days after the attacks and, almost as quickly, were shot down. The meeting was reconfirmed by Czech officials several days later and promptly discredited with a series of leaks to journalists from unnamed intelligence officials. This cycle continued for months, and when it ended, establishment journalists and the skeptics who fed them had won. *Newsweek* dismissed reports of the meeting as "hoary" and the *New York Times* concluded it "almost certainly never took place."

Nonetheless, the alleged encounter was the subject of dozens of meetings at the highest levels of the U.S. government. International diplomats and spy chiefs shuttled from city to city to compare notes. The CIA set up a special team to examine reports of the contact. News coverage of the issue would fill several thick books.

Some of the intelligence makes the alleged meeting seem unlikely. Although Atta often traveled on his own passport, making it easy for U.S. authorities to retrace his steps, there is no indication that he left the United States during the time he is alleged to have been in Prague. And some Czech officials who have emphatically confirmed the meeting in their public statements are somewhat less confident in private interviews.

But other reports suggest that the meeting did, in fact, take place. An informant for the Czech Republic's domestic intelligence service, the BIS, claims to have witnessed the meeting. Atta had been to Prague three times since his first trip in 1994. Ten months before his alleged meeting with Iraqi intelligence agent Ahmed Khalil Ibrahim Samir al Ani, he went to great lengths and overcame several obstacles to stop in Prague en route from Germany to the United States. A large sum of money was deposited in Atta's Sun Trust bank account shortly after that first trip. According to a top secret Pentagon report, Czech intelligence reported that al Ani "ordered the IIS [Iraqi Intelligence Service] finance officer to issue Atta funds from IIS financial holdings in the Prague office." The surveillance photography from a U.S. government building in Prague shows al Ani casing the structure, accompanied by an unidentified man who appears to have roughly the same build as Atta. No fewer than five high-ranking Czech officials have publicly confirmed that the meeting occurred.

In spite of this, prominent stories in *Newsweek* and the *New*

York Times have suggested that the meeting did not take place. The FBI, according to accounts in both publications, has documentary evidence proving that such a meeting not only did not happen but that such a meeting *could not* have happened.

But no such evidence exists. And CIA director George Tenet has privately told associates and journalists that despite the lack of clear-cut proof, he believes the Atta meeting happened. Although journalists considered the matter dead and buried, the so-called Prague connection was still very much a live issue in late January 2004, when Tenet met with the man who headed the investigation for the Czechs, interior minister Stanislav Gross. A month later, in an appearance before the Senate Intelligence Committee, Tenet said that his agency hadn't gathered evidence to either prove or disprove the meeting.

So what, if anything, happened in Prague?

The story begins not in 2001, but in the spring of 1994. And it involves not one plot, but two.

From 1951 until the end of the cold war, radio broadcasts funded by the U.S. government and transmitted from Munich, Germany, provided a pipeline of news and anti-Communist propaganda into the Soviet Union and the eastern and central European nations under Soviet domination. In 1994, Czech president Vaclav Havel invited Radio Free Europe/Radio Liberty, the agency responsible for those broadcasts, to relocate to Prague.

The move made sense, in both financial and ideological terms. In the United States, the radio networks had been increasingly criticized for profligate spending and an uncertain mission. The collapse of the Soviet Union, critics argued, rendered the broadcasts irrelevant and anachronistic. These arguments met fierce resistance from congressional internationalists like Senator Joseph Biden, a Democrat from Delaware.

As the debate intensified, Biden received crucial support from former dissidents in the former Soviet bloc. The government of Latvia nominated the network for the Nobel Peace Prize in 1990. Czech president Havel, an underground playwright who agitated for decades against Soviet oppression, was a stalwart supporter of the programs. A move from Munich to Prague, where the dollar was very strong, would allow the network to dramatically cut its costs, and Havel added another incentive by offering to rent the services a building for just 1 Czech crown—about 25 cents—a month.

On March 10, 1995, the new Radio Free Europe/Radio Liberty broadcast for the first time from Prague. The following year, on July 4, First Lady Hillary Clinton visited the broadcast center, now housed in a former Communist Party parliament building located at the geographic heart of Prague, to praise its work. The new headquarters, she told her audience, was "an emblem of the political, economic, and social transformations that have taken place in Central Europe."

In due time, the headquarters would come to symbolize changes the Clinton administration and many in Congress hoped to achieve in the Middle East, too. By early 1998, tensions between Saddam Hussein and the UN weapons inspectors once again dominated the news. The diplomatic dancing continued for several months, and on August 5, 1998, the Iraqi regime announced that it was suspending cooperation with UN inspectors. As another round of negotiations between the Iraqis and the UN began, officials in Washington discussed other measures to deal with Saddam. One of the options, establishing a radio service that would transmit broadcast news and opinion into Iraq, looked promising.

But the Czechs had some concerns. Permitting anti-Saddam broadcasts to go out from Prague, critics argued, would make the capital a target for terrorist attacks. The Czech public agreed, with polls showing a majority opposed to the plan.

Seeking a compromise, the Czechs asked their American partners to find an out-of-the-way location for the new service. The Americans, in what some Czechs considered an act of bad faith, proposed a building in an upscale residential area in Prague. "It had a kindergarten on one side and a kindergarten on the other side," says an official familiar with the negotiations. The alternative site was nixed, and the Czechs, with reservations, eventually agreed to house the broadcast in the Wenceslas Square headquarters, where Radio Free Europe/Radio Liberty was located.

Radio Free Iraq, along with a sister service that broadcast into Iran, went on air for the first time on October 30, 1998. The Czechs increased security around the building, hastily reinforcing the perimeter with additional Jersey barriers and armed guards. That same day, in the face of continued Iraqi defiance of UN weapons inspectors, the UN Security Council announced a plan to review sanctions against the regime.

Saddam was not happy about either of these developments. The next day he announced that Iraq would indefinitely suspend cooperation with UN weapons inspectors. The Iranians weren't happy, either, and within days recalled their diplomatic staff from Prague. For reasons that would later become obvious, Iraq did not.

In Iraq, the initial public reaction to the broadcasts was in-difference interrupted by bursts of outrage. A commentator from the government-run Radio Baghdad scoffed at his new competitor. "If they think they can influence the morale and fighting spirit of the Iraqi people, or their solidarity with its courageous leadership, the Americans are kidding them-selves."

On November 2, 1998, three days after Radio Free Iraq first went on the air, Iraqi foreign minister Mohammed Saeed al Sahaf—who would come to be known to the world as "Bagh-dad Bob"—warned the Czechs in an address to the Iraqi Na-tional Assembly.

With respect to the question on Iraqi government contacts with the current government of Prague regarding the lat-ter's approval to have a poisonous radio station—led by the Americans and the Zionists—broadcast from the Czech ter-ritories; as I have pointed out earlier, as soon as the U.S. idea first sprang up we contacted the Czechs and explained things to them and warned them against something like this. Eight members of the Czech government approved the idea and seven opposed it. It was the vote of one person that granted approval to the U.S. request. We have ex-plained to them very clearly that such a step is against our common interests and against the two countries' bilateral ties. We also explained that such a decision will cost the Czech side huge losses . . . we have already started taking measures and informed them [the Czechs] how our bilat-eral ties will be affected and how economic and trade exchange even within the framework of the Memorandum of Understanding will be affected. We told them that this will have even worse repercussions in the future.

Some observers, including several in the Czech government, were worried that Iraqi predictions of "huge losses" to the Czechs and warnings of "worse repercussions in the future" might refer not to trade but to human life. But Sahaf's remarks clearly came in the context of his broader discussion of bilateral trade and were mostly ignored as harmless bluster.

Six days later though, on November 8, 1998, a commentator on Iraqi television—the regime's mouthpiece—warned of the "jihad spirit" of Iraqis. "This new station will only transmit poison, lies and cheap political intrigues. Announcing this new station clearly reflects U.S. disappointment, failure, and incompetence to undermine the patriotism of the genuine Iraqis, as well as their special, deep relationship with their historic leadership under mujahid leader Saddam Husayn," the commentator read. "The great people of Iraq faced—and will face—this hostile propaganda with contempt and absolute rejection . . . The Americans will be deluding themselves if they think that, with this new propagandist trumpet, they can influence the stand, morale, and jihad spirit of the people of Iraq or undermine their firm conviction in and splendid unity with their brave, faithful leadership."

The worrisome jihad reference was a sign of things to come. Three days after this statement, Saddam's National Baath Party put out a message of its own. Hostility between the Iraqi regime and the United States was more inflamed than it had been for months. The message—a call to the Arab nation to the "highest level of jihad"—was direct and chilling.

"O sons of our glorious and mujahid Arab nation, the inheritors of civilizations and the eternal message: the enemies of Iraq, the enemies of Arabism and Islam, are planning to carry out a new aggression against Iraq. Therefore, the eyes of Arabs today are focused on Iraq, the arena of jihad, which is facing fateful challenges, the unjust blockade, and the possibilities of the premeditated aggression by the United States and its tyrant Zionist ally, with a spirit of jihad, steadfastness, patience, and creative struggle . . ."

The statement urged "steadfastness in the historic" Mother of All Battles and called for jihad strugglers to carry out "unprecedented heroisms." It warned of the "Zionist spirit" of the U.S. government and declared:

The answer that suits the nature of the challenge requires opening all doors of struggle. All living capabilities of the nation should be directed toward the unity of the pan-Arab confrontation and toward escalating the struggle to the highest level of jihad . . .

The escalation of the confrontation and the disclosure of its dimensions and the aggressive intentions now require an organized, planned, influential, and conclusive enthusiasm against the U.S. interests. There is no doubt that the power of the nation is stronger than that of its enemy. The spiritual values of the nation have a bigger effect than that of the enemies' technological power and can better serve the consciences of peoples and the human values . . .

O the sons of the nation of strugglers and martyrs, the Arabs are standing at a big crossroads in their history. They should make use of this opportunity and pay the price for this chance. They should proceed with the spirit of martyrs toward their objectives of liberation and defend their national entity. There is no method, approach, or force, which can be equal to this hostile and barbaric U.S. spirit. Therefore, the Arab nation should take the historic initiative and shoulder the responsibility of jihad and struggle in this new confrontation in order to preserve the liberated Arab base, which has put the Arab nation on the road to the future, the liberation of Palestine, and the unity and awakening of the nation.

The directive was signed, "The National Command of the Arab Socialist Ba'ath Party, on 11th November 1998."

Hours later President Clinton, in a Veterans Day speech at Arlington National Cemetery, countered the warning. "We continue to hope, indeed pray, that Saddam will comply. But we must be prepared to act if he does not." Both President Clinton and Saddam Hussein met with their respective military leaders. U.S. forces in the region prepared for an attack, and Iraqi forces were repositioned to meet them.

Iraq's fiery rhetoric was more than just talk. Even as the public back-and-forth continued, Saddam's intelligence service secretly set in motion plans to back up its threats. The Mukhabarat, acting through its intelligence chief in Prague, would indeed "escalate the struggle to the highest levels of jihad" with "an organized, planned, influential, and conclusive enthusiasm against the U.S. interests." The target: Radio Free Europe/Radio Liberty.

In the fall of 1998, Saddam's intelligence service wired approximately $150,000 to its satellite headquarters in Prague, according to an account by the man on the receiving end. The money came with specific instructions: blow up the broadcast headquarters of Radio Free Iraq. Jabir Salim, the top Iraqi intelligence official in central Europe, was told to find a young Islamic radical willing to commit the "martyrdom operation"—driving a truck filled with explosives into the side of the building that housed the American broadcasting outlets. That task itself would not be difficult. Finding someone to carry it out would be.

The building is located nearly atop a well-traveled highway, says one top Czech official, "and the Prague subway runs directly beneath it." Blowing it up, he says, "would be simple, really."

Some accounts published in the European press contend that Western intelligence services were working to "flip" Salim—to recruit him as a double agent. Others suggest that even as the Iraqis plotted, Salim was sharing this information with the West.

Regardless of which version is accurate, the plot was exposed during the first week of November when an unnamed Czech official told a group of reporters that Czech intelligence had learned that an "Islamic terrorist" planned to bomb the Radio Free Europe/Radio Liberty building.

Salim stopped coming to work at the Iraqi embassy at some point in mid-December. The Czechs, who were closely monitoring his activities, observed him emptying his Prague apartment. Salim told the other employees at the embassy that he had to take his sick daughter to Austria for medical attention.

But Salim never went to Austria. He defected with the help of British intelligence, first to Germany, then to England, where he disclosed details of the plan to bomb the U.S. government building to British foreign intelligence.

A Czech source says that Salim's boss, the former chargé d'affaires at the embassy in Prague, was recalled to Baghdad. Rumors in diplomatic circles, he says, held that the Iraqi "didn't survive his meeting with Saddam."

The Salim story, curiously, got hardly a mention in the American media. Critics of the Iraq War often claim that Iraq has not so much as attempted anti-American terrorism since 1993. Leaving aside the question of whether Iraq may have had a yet undiscovered role in attacks in the 1990s, the story of Jabir Salim suggests that the Iraqi regime continued to plot against American interests.

Salim sneaked out of Prague as the Clinton administration launched "Operation Desert Fox," on December 16, 1998, a seventy-hour bombing campaign that struck key facilities involved in Iraq's weapons of mass destruction program. Radio Free Iraq increased its broadcasts into Iraq from two to four hours daily. The Iraqis were furious.

Iraq took two months to name Salim's replacement: Ahmed Khalil Ibrahim Samir al Ani.

According to David Rose, a contributing writer to *Vanity Fair* who has reported extensively on Iraq–al Qaeda connections, al Ani was known to his friends as "Abu Amin," which means "the father of honesty." Al Ani was "one of Iraq's most highly decorated intelligence officers: a Special Forces veteran who organized killings behind Iranian lines" during the Iran-Iraq War. Al Ani, Rose reported, in the November 11, 2001, edition of London's *Observer*, "went on to a senior post in the unit known as 'M8'—the department for special operations, such as sabotage, terrorism, and murder."

Al Ani and his superiors in Iraqi intelligence knew he would be the subject of close surveillance. "We expected to watch him and he expected to be watched," says a top Czech official.

Monitoring al Ani would not be difficult. Prague has a Muslim population of some twenty thousand, and of that number an estimated one hundred were Iraqis. The city didn't even have a mosque until the First Islamic Center and Mosque was founded in 2001. The Iraqi embassy in Prague, during al Ani's time there, employed only five people.

And al Ani didn't even try to hide. From the moment he arrived in Prague, he was a well-known presence. He frequented Arab-owned bakeries and two Lebanese restaurants, often trying to provoke the owners and patrons into political discussions. "He was very aggressive, a provocateur," says a Czech official familiar with intelligence on al Ani.

It didn't take long for al Ani to turn his attention to Radio Free Iraq. "We have lots of pictures of al Ani taking photographs," says Tom Dine, president of Radio Free Europe/Radio Liberty. "We used to call him 'The Shell' because he wore a T-shirt or a jacket with a shell on the back."

He also began to seek out the station's employees. "It doesn't do you much good to report back to Baghdad about the activities of people in bakeries," says the Czech official. "He started to harass the employees of RFE/RL."

Curiously, al Ani wasn't the only one casing the building. Dine describes a steady stream of Arabs monitoring and photographing RFE/RL headquarters. "They all drove Mercedes," he recalls. "They parked in the public parking lot across the street and walked into the National Museum, across from us. We would give our Czech counterparts photographs of license plates, people—always Arabs—and anything else we got."

The Czechs would trace the license plates, Dine explains, linking the cars to suspicious figures from a number of countries. "Egyptians, Yemenis, and I think one Saudi. The owner of the cars would be an Arab of some kind and would be married to a Czech woman," says Dine. "Of course, the owner of the car always said he had loaned it to someone else and had no idea who was using it."

Were they working with the Iraqis? That's unclear. Under Communist rule until 1989, Prague was known to be the hub for Soviet training of Middle Eastern terrorists. Dine speculates that some of these shadowy figures might have been holdovers.

The security forces at RFE/RL actively sought them out, says Dine, at times following them "right into the National Museum, up the stairs, to the window. We would be taking photographs of them taking photographs of us." Those pictures were turned over to Czech counterintelligence.

Back in Baghdad, Iraqi officials were still angry about Radio Free Iraq. Hynek Kmonicek, who was then the Czech Republic's deputy foreign minister, saw this firsthand when he went to Iraq in January 2000. Kmonicek, regarded as one of the Czech Republic's foremost experts on the Arab world, went to Baghdad with a clear mission. During the cold war, Czechs had built some 60 percent of Iraq's oil refineries, and now the Iraqis wanted Czech experts, those who knew the most about these projects, to help update those facilities. The Czechs, in return, wanted the Iraqis to recognize the breakup of the former Czechoslovakia. Iraq was one of a handful of countries that had not formally acknowledged the new governments in the Czech Republic and Slovakia, preventing the Czechs from legally recovering debts that the Iraqis had piled up during the Czechoslovak Communist era.

Kmonicek says he had worked out the outline of an agreement with the Iraqis even before leaving Prague for Baghdad. The Czechs would agree to help with the refineries, and Iraq would recognize the Czech Republic. Upon arrival, however, Kmonicek discovered that the terms of the deal had changed rather dramatically.

Radio Free Iraq must be closed down, Kmonicek was told by Taha Yasin Ramadan, Saddam's vice president, or the deal was off. Kmonicek protested, and the discussion quickly became heated.

"He was shouting at me," Kmonicek recalls. "I was shouting at him." Ramadan scolded his Czech visitor, saying, "But you were our friends." Kmonicek explained that Radio Free Iraq was a not a Czech broadcast and that the transmitters were not even physically located in his country. He warned Ramadan not to treat the Czechs with disrespect, saying that the Czech Republic "isn't Belarus." Ramadan was furious. "You are the worst enemy," he said. "You are the worst enemy. Worse than Belarus. You betrayed us."

The meeting was abruptly cut short, but "I kept shouting," Kmonicek says. "All the way into the limo, which I knew must be bugged, I kept shouting." He was eager to return to Prague.

Mohamed Atta, later that spring, was also eager to get to Prague. Atta, an Egyptian student living in Hamburg, made plans to visit the Czech capital by applying for a visa in Bonn, Germany, on May 26, 2000. He was apparently one day late. His subsequent behavior suggests that Atta needed the visa for a trip scheduled for May 30, 2000. The visa wasn't ready. But Atta took a Lufthansa flight to Prague-Ružyne Airport anyway.

Without a visa, Atta could go no farther than the arrival/departure terminal, and remained in this section of the airport for nearly six hours. According to journalist Edward Jay Epstein, a contributor to *Slate* magazine, Atta—and presumably the person he was there to meet—managed to avoid the security cameras arrayed throughout the area for all but a few minutes of his brief stay. "From this visaless round trip, Czech intelligence inferred that Atta had a meeting on May 30 that could not wait, even a day—and that whoever arranged it was probably familiar with the transit lounge's surveillance."

But Atta wasn't done in Prague. Three days later, after picking up his new visa in Bonn, he boarded a bus in Frankfurt bound for Prague. After the approximately seven-hour trip, Atta disappeared in Prague for almost twenty-four hours. Czech officials report that they cannot find evidence of his staying in a hotel under his own name, suggesting he stayed somewhere under an assumed name or stayed in a private home. Atta flew to Newark, New Jersey, the following day.

None of this caused the Czechs any concern at the time, of

course, since neither they nor anyone else had reason to be suspicious of Atta. These discoveries came only when the Czechs launched an intelligence investigation into Atta's activities after the September 11 attacks.

In the meantime, the Czechs kept a watchful eye on al Ani, the Iraqi intelligence agent operating out of the embassy. There was no doubt that al Ani was doing intelligence work for Saddam. He had been in the Czech Republic for nearly a year, and he had yet to attend any diplomatic function in his ostensible capacity as the embassy's number two. He was seen numerous times near the Radio Free Europe/Radio Liberty headquarters taking photographs of the building.

The Czechs decided to issue a formal warning. Kmonicek called Kamal al Tikriti, the chargé d'affaires at the Iraqi embassy (according to some, a distant cousin of Saddam) and suggested that al Ani "issue a visa and pretend at least to do some diplomatic work."

Al Tikriti, who didn't speak a language other than his native Arabic, was "absolutely terrified," says Kmonicek. "It was strange. He was very afraid of his number two."

Despite the warning, nothing changed. Al Ani was as active as ever. "He behaved as if he wanted to be kicked out," recalls Kmonicek.

In early April, the Czech intelligence service, the BIS, received a tip from one of its part-time informants. Al Ani was scheduled to meet a "student from Hamburg," who might be dangerous, at some point in the next several days. In the end, there may have been two meetings on April 9, 2001. The account of the first meeting comes from the single Arab informant who, after the September 11 attacks, identified the "student" as Mohamed Atta. Al Ani met the student at a restaurant outside Prague.

A second sighting is what concerned Czech intelligence officials and ultimately led them to expel al Ani. They had long feared that al Ani would succeed where his predecessor failed—in recruiting a suicide bomber to take out Radio Free Iraq—and their anxiety heightened when al Ani was seen with the student outside the Radio Free Europe headquarters. Various press reports have claimed that the Americans have videotape or still photographs of the meeting. Asked generally about photographic evidence, a senior Czech official says, "I have not seen any videotape of the meeting." And photos? "I have not seen any videotape of the meeting."

The Czechs were coy about the photographs, but Tom Dine is not. The photos offer a clear shot of al Ani, but the image of his companion is unclear. "It doesn't look like the [photographs of] Atta we saw on September 12, 2001," he says.

The Czechs did not follow the student. But Kmonicek and his boss, foreign minister Jan Kavan, were sufficiently concerned about his activities that they decided to declare al Ani persona non grata (PNG), a change in his diplomatic status that would result in his expulsion.

On April 21, 2001, before they notified the Iraqis, Czech counterintelligence briefed the CIA station chief in Prague about the meeting between the student and al Ani and about their decision to "PNG" the Iraqi spy.

The next day, Kmonicek phoned the Iraqi embassy to inform the chargé d'affaires that al Ani had just twenty-four hours to leave the country. The Czechs were concerned that, given time, he would attempt to notify his contacts—perhaps including the student—of his departure.

Later that same day, al Ani's boss, Kamal al Tikriti, called with a "big wish." The top Iraqi embassy official was once again terrified. He wanted the Czechs to give al Ani more time. Al Ani was having trouble getting a travel visa to return to Iraq, something Kmonicek tried to rectify quickly. Al Ani was gone forty-eight hours later. Kmonicek informed the Iraqis that as a gesture of goodwill, he would keep the entire episode quiet.

Four days later, on April 26, 2001, as Kmonicek was traveling in Tunisia, the Iraqis got their revenge, letting the world know that an employee of the Czech embassy in Baghdad had been expelled in response to the removal of al Ani. The Czechs, having informed the CIA about al Ani's activities, considered the matter closed.

The meeting was largely ignored until shortly after September 11, when the Czechs' Arab informant, having seen news coverage linking Atta to the attacks, immediately called to inform them that Atta was the man who had met with al Ani the previous spring. The Czechs, in turn, quickly notified the CIA.

The Czechs hedged their report, telling both the CIA and the FBI that there was a "possible chance" the student who had met with al Ani was Atta. All parties agreed that it was wise to keep the report from the public. But on September 18, 2001, the sketchy details of the alleged meeting were reported in a short article by the Associated Press. Other news outlets confirmed the story and, within days, the al Ani–Atta meeting emerged as evidence that Iraq might have been involved in the

September 11 attacks. Almost as quickly, anonymous investigators and former intelligence officials began casting doubt on the meeting and on potential Iraqi involvement in the September 11 attacks. A report on CNN on September 19, 2001, cited U.S. officials with knowledge of the meeting saying Iraq was not involved.

The Czechs were not happy. Reporters hounding them "forced us to say 'Yes' or 'No' before we were ready," says one Czech official involved in the investigation.

In an interview on October 16, 2001, with the *New York Times*, Czech interior minister Stanislav Gross said that his government could confirm "only one visit [to Prague] in the summer" of 2000.

The Iraqis were quick to deny any connection. "Iraq has absolutely no link with what happened or with the groups the United States accuses of being responsible," said foreign minister Naji Sabri in Baghdad. "How has the U.S. administration been able, just minutes after the incident, to accuse Arab and Islamic parties?"

"We are not waging war against the United States outside Iraq," said Iraqi vice premier Tariq Aziz, at a press conference in Baghdad on October 17, 2001. "We don't believe in that. . . . We are prepared to resist continuous American aggression against Iraq within the territory of Iraq. We don't need bin Laden for that because we are capable of doing it."

Aziz initially denied reports of the Atta–al Ani meeting. "This meeting did not take place," Aziz said. "It is a lie. We checked with him: 'Did you ever meet somebody called Atta?' "

One reporter then asked if it was possible that Atta met

with al Ani using a different name. Aziz shifted his explanation.

"Even if such an incident had taken place, it doesn't mean anything," Aziz explained. "Any diplomat in any mission might meet people in a restaurant here or there and talk to them, which is meaningless. If that person turned out to be something else, that doesn't mean that he had a connection with what that person did later."

When journalists at the press conference asked to speak with al Ani directly, Aziz dismissed the idea. "This accusation is ridiculous."

One week later, on October 26, 2001, Stanislav Gross, whose agency oversees the Czech intelligence service, made a statement to reporters about Atta's activities in Prague that appeared to reverse his position from ten days earlier. "We can confirm now that during his next [spring 2001] trip to the Czech Republic he did have contact with an officer of the Iraqi intelligence, Mr. Ahmed Khalil Ibrahim Samir al Ani," said Gross. "Details of their meeting are being investigated."

In an interview broadcast two weeks later on CNN, Czech prime minister Milos Zeman confirmed the meeting, but added to the confusion by claiming knowledge of its contents. "Atta contacted some Iraq agent, not to prepare the terrorist attack" on September 11, "but to prepare a terrorist attack on just the building of Radio Free Europe." Top Czech officials were privately critical of Zeman's statement, pointing out that without audio surveillance, there was no way to know what was said at the meeting. "Zeman just wanted to get on CNN," says one official familiar with the controversy.

In time, three additional high-ranking Czech officials would confirm the meeting: Martin Palous, ambassador to the United States and previously deputy foreign minister; Kmonicek, ambassador to the United Nations; and Jiri Ruzek, the intelligence chief.

Despite all this, some U.S. officials and many journalists remained skeptical.

On December 16, 2001, the *New York Times* reported that American officials in Washington "said the diplomat was a minor functionary who happens to have the same last name as a more important Iraqi intelligence agent."

But by early February, the *Times* was saying that "senior American intelligence officials have concluded that the meeting between Mr. Atta and the Iraqi officer, Ahmed Khalil Ibrahim Samir al-Ani, did take place. But they say they do not believe that the meeting provides enough evidence to tie Iraq to the Sept. 11 attacks."

And later that spring, just over a year after the alleged meeting, reporters were accusing the administration of politicizing intelligence. "The story behind the purported Atta-Iraqi meeting is nonetheless an illuminating window into the murky world of intelligence in the war on terrorism—and how easily facts can become distorted for political purposes," wrote *Newsweek*'s Michael Isikoff. The *Newsweek* article, first published on April 28, 2002, quoted a "senior U.S. law enforcement official" saying, "We looked at this real hard because, obviously, if it were true, it would be huge. But nothing has matched up." Isikoff allowed that new information suggesting a link could turn up, but concluded, "for now, at least, the much-touted 'Prague connection' appears to be an intriguing, but embarrassing, mistake."

On May 1, 2002, *Washington Post* reporter Walter Pincus followed up on the *Newsweek* story by citing a senior administration official. Pincus wrote that "there is no evidence" of the Prague meeting, something his source determined "eliminates a once-suggested link between the terrorist attack and the government of President Saddam Hussein."

The Czechs, the original source of the intelligence, swiftly and decisively rejected the news reports. As Interior Minister Gross had told a Prague newspaper, "I believe the counterintelligence services more than I believe journalists. I draw on the Security Information Service [BIS] information and I see no reason why I should not believe it." Gross checked with his intelligence chief to determine whether any fresh evidence had come to light that might discredit the earlier reporting. The answer, he said, was no. "I consider the case closed."

It was not. The public back-and-forth over the Prague connection continued throughout the summer and well into the fall. On October 21, 2002, the *New York Times* reported in a front-page piece that Czech president Vaclav Havel "quietly told the White House he has concluded that there is no evidence to confirm earlier reports" of the meeting. The Czechs continue to deny Havel telephoned the White House to distance his government from the controversy. "The phone call never happened," says a senior Czech official. "It never happened." The *Times* ran a news piece two days later quoting Havel's spokesman. "The president did not call the White

House about this. The president never spoke with any American government official about Atta, not with Bush, not with anyone else."

Nonetheless, the *Times* editorial page weighed in on the same day just eleven pages later, under the headline "The Illusory Prague Connection." The editorial claimed that the original news report confirmed that the meeting "almost certainly never took place."

The conventional wisdom was well on its way to solidifying: the Prague connection was bogus. Several news reports even claimed that the FBI had documentary evidence placing Atta in the United States at the time of the alleged meeting. A *Newsweek* article on June 9, 2003, stated flatly, "Atta was traveling at the time between Florida and Virginia Beach, Va. (The bureau [FBI] had his rental car and hotel receipts.)"

But that reporting tells only part of the story. The context is important. Although the FBI has a steady stream of paperwork on Atta's movements and financial transactions in the months leading up to the September 11 attacks, there is a gap of at least three days in the paper trail, and that gap coincides with the time Atta is alleged to have been in Prague. In fact, according to two U.S. government sources, the only documents potentially placing Atta in the United States at the time of the alleged meeting are cell phone records. Interesting, but hardly conclusive. Many of the hijackers shared cell phones, and investigators believe it's possible that someone other than Atta was using the phone at the time.

As CIA director George Tenet's various public comments suggest, the Prague connection is hardly the dead issue that reports in the U.S. media might suggest. There are several unresolved questions. According to Czech officials familiar with the investigation, Atta's bank accounts in both the United States and Germany received several large deposits—totaling almost $100,000—shortly after he left Prague on June 2, 2000. Although many of the transfers into Atta's accounts were easily traced back to the sender, this one was not. Why?

The Feith memo appears to take the financial transactions much further. "The Czech counterintelligence service reported that the Sept. 11 hijacker Atta met with the former Iraqi intelligence chief in Prague, al Ani, on several occasions. During one of these meetings al Ani ordered the IIS [Iraqi Intelligence Service] finance officer to issue Atta funds from IIS financial holdings in the Prague office." CIA reporting included in the Feith memo claims that Czech intelligence reports not two, but four trips to Prague by Atta. "CIA can confirm two Atta visits to Prague—in Dec 1994 and in June 2000; data surrounding the other two—on 26 Oct 1999 and 9 April 2001—is complicated and sometimes contradictory and CIA and FBI cannot confirm Atta met with IIS."

The Pentagon summary of the reporting from the Czechs is troubling and self-contradictory. Czechs familiar with the intelligence cannot confirm that al Ani ever ordered the Iraqi Intelligence Service funds to Atta. And absent listening devices, it's unclear how anyone would know that the order to transfer funds, if it happened, took place "during one of these meetings."

Still, there are several details of the investigation that have never been publicly revealed. According to Bush administration sources, they are compelling enough to have convinced several top officials on the Bush administration's national security team that the April 9, 2001, meeting took place. National security adviser Condoleezza Rice strongly believes that al Ani met with Atta. Vice President Dick Cheney is less certain, but thinks it more likely than not that the two got together. Deputy secretary of defense Paul Wolfowitz, often portrayed as the most hawkish among top administration officials, is more skeptical.

Most interesting, however, is CIA director George Tenet. He says in private the same thing he says in public: the meeting cannot be proven or disproven on the available evidence. But when pressed, Tenet has told associates and some journalists that he, too, thinks that Atta met with Iraqi intelligence.

The best sources are not exactly in a position to be helpful. Al Ani, the Iraqi intelligence officer now in U.S. custody, naturally denies meeting with Atta. And Mohamed Atta, of course, is dead.

CHAPTER TEN

ACT GLOBALLY

On October 2, 2002, shortly before 8:30 P.M., Sergeant First Class Mark Wayne Jackson and a fellow Special Forces soldier stopped at a café and karaoke bar just outside the gate of Camp Enrile Malagutay. The men were part of a team of 260 soldiers involved in training exercises near Zamboanga City, a poor, heavily Muslim town in Mindanao, an island in the southern Philippines. Terrorists from Abu Sayyaf, a gang of thieves and kidnappers long affiliated with al Qaeda, were not happy about the American presence. One week earlier, Abu Sayyaf leaders promised a campaign of terror aimed at the "enemies of Islam"—Westerners and the Filipinos who make common cause with them.

Many American soldiers had befriended the owners of the small restaurant, which had become a favorite for the U.S. troops stationed there. The café sits among the palm trees in the middle of a small strip of shops, along the dusty road leading to the base.

No one paid much attention when a young Filipino man parked his Honda motorcycle in front of the café and began examining its tank. Seconds later, a homemade bomb inside the motorcycle exploded, sending nails in every direction and killing the motorcyclist almost instantly. The front of the café was blown away. Six nearby stores were damaged. One shop lost its roof. The nails that had been packed into the bomb littered the ground.

Soldiers at the base had assumed the alarm was yet another drill. They arrived to find Jackson dead and his companion seriously wounded.

Eyewitnesses identified the bomber as a member of Abu Sayyaf, an al Qaeda–linked group founded with the help of Osama bin Laden's brother-in-law. Abu Sayyaf was created as something of an umbrella organization designed to unite smaller, disparate groups of Islamic radicals into a stronger, more deadly operation. It didn't work. Despite cash infusions from al Qaeda and training for its fighters in Afghanistan, Abu Sayyaf radicals kept mostly to themselves, conducting predominantly small-scale attacks and kidnappings for ransom.

Exactly one week after the café attack, Filipino authorities found an unexploded bomb on the playground of the San Roque Elementary School, also in Zamboanga City. The bomb was to have been detonated by a cell phone. Filipino investigators analyzed the calls to and from that phone, and several piqued their interest, including calls to and from two Abu Sayyaf leaders. But one call that stood out had been placed seventeen hours after the bombing that killed Sergeant Jackson, to an Iraqi intelligence agent named Hisham Hussein, who was working as the second secretary at the Iraqi embassy in Manila.

On February 14, 2003, Hisham Hussein was asked to leave the Philippines for conduct incompatible with his diplomatic status. Officials there had been watching Hussein for months and had stepped up their monitoring after discovering his contacts with Abu Sayyaf. "He was surveilled, and we found out he was in contact with Abu Sayyaf and also pro-Iraqi demonstrators," says a Philippine government source. "[Philippine intelligence] was able to monitor their cell phone calls. [Abu Sayyaf leaders] called [Hussein] right after the bombing. They were always talking."

Andrea Domingo, immigration commissioner for the Philippines, said "studying the movements and activities" of Iraqi intelligence assets in the country, including radical Islamists, revealed an "established network" of terrorists headed by Hisham Hussein. A subsequent analysis of Iraq embassy phone records indicated that Hussein had been in regular contact with Abu Sayyaf leaders both before and after the Zamboanga City bombing.

There was more. Hamsinaji Sali, an Abu Sayyaf leader, had claimed that Iraq had provided the group with arms and funding, 1 million pesos—about $20,000—each year since 2000. After learning about the extensive contacts between Hussein and Abu Sayyaf, once dubious intelligence officials gave new credence to Sali's claims.

Hussein also met with members of the New People's Army, a communist opposition group included on the State Department's list of foreign terrorist groups, in his office at the Iraqi embassy. The Philippine National Police later uncovered documents in an NPA compound that it says prove the Iraqi embassy had provided funding for the group.

Two additional Iraq embassy employees were expelled days later, as were several Iraqi nationals suspected of collaborating with Islamic terrorists. The expulsions came on the heels of Colin Powell's presentation to the United Nations Security Council and shortly before the war in Iraq.

Matthew Daley, U.S. deputy assistant secretary of state for East Asian and Pacific affairs, articulated the concerns about Abu Sayyaf in congressional testimony on March 26, 2003. "We're concerned that they have what I would call operational links to Iraqi intelligence services . . . there is good reason to believe that a member of the Abu Sayyaf Group who has been involved in terrorist activities was in direct contact with an IIS officer in the Iraqi Embassy in Manila."

One month after Daley's testimony, reporters discovered documents in Iraq that bolstered the Bush administration's prewar claims that Saddam was supporting Islamic extremists, including al Qaeda. As noted, one 1992 document shows that the Mukhabarat believed bin Laden was an asset in close contact with Iraqi intelligence in Syria. Reporters from the *Toronto Star* and *London Telegraph* also found papers that describe a series of meetings in 1998 between a senior al Qaeda representative and Iraqi intelligence.

There is more. "A cache of files recovered from the bombed-out headquarters of Iraq's intelligence agency shows Saddam Hussein's regime had links to an Islamist terror group in Africa—and had corresponded about opening a Baghdad training camp for the group," wrote Philip Smucker and Faye Bowers in the *Christian Science Monitor* on April 18, 2003.

The series of letters were sent in 2001 to the Iraqi chargé d'affaires in Nairobi, Kenya, from Bekkah Abdul Nassir, leader of the al Qaeda–linked Allied Democratic Forces in Uganda.

They call for access to a training camp in Baghdad, "headquarters for the international Holy warrior network," to establish an "international mujahideen team whose special mission will be to smuggle arms on a global scale to holy warriors fighting against U.S., British, and Israeli influences in Africa, the Middle East, and Far East." Nassir indicated that the ADF had operatives "on the ground working in Baghdad" ready to undertake "actions to paralyze and control the hostile intelligence actions of the CIA, the Pentagon, and Mossad [Israel intelligence] and MI6 [British intelligence]."

The *Monitor* reporters were careful to indicate that there is no evidence the Iraqi regime acted on the plans. But one letter mentions agreement on an "appropriate budget," something the reporters took to imply "either that money figures were indeed discussed at some point, or that ADF officials thought they soon would be."

If the reports on Iraqi support for the ADF were suggestive but inconclusive, the same cannot be said for another al Qaeda affiliate, Ansar al Islam.

CHAPTER ELEVEN

ANSAR AL ISLAM

On September 1, 2001, ten days before the attacks on America, terrorists in northern Iraq held a ceremony to celebrate the establishment of a new organization. The group was small; the most reliable estimates place its membership at six hundred to seven hundred fighters. But it brought together a number of smaller radical Islamic groups under the auspices of a big one: Jund al Islam. At another ceremony in December, the fledgling group changed its name to one that Americans would hear repeatedly in news dispatches from postwar Iraq: Ansar al Islam.

From the beginning the new group had direct ties to Osama bin Laden. Abu Zubaydah, a senior al Qaeda operative now in U.S. custody, told interrogators that bin Laden had provided start-up money for Jund al Islam. Numerous other al Qaeda detainees have corroborated his account. When U.S. troops stormed the group's camp days after the first bombs fell in the Iraq War, they found copies of bomb-making manuals and videotapes identical to those found in al Qaeda camps during the war in Afghanistan. The ties to al Qaeda were never in dispute.

More controversial, however, were Ansar al Islam's connections with the Iraqi regime. Certainly Saddam had every incentive to cooperate with the Islamists. They shared a common enemy, the Kurdish forces that had been an ongoing source of trouble for the Iraqi regime. But did he?

According to detainees from both Iraqi intelligence and Ansar al Islam, he did. The support came in the form of financial payments and arms. And the third-ranking official in Ansar al Islam was an Iraqi intelligence agent who reported to top Mukhabarat officials and, according to one detainee, met personally with Saddam Hussein four or five times.

The intelligence on Ansar al Islam comes from a wide variety of sources and was reported by several different intelligence agencies. The accounts of the group's hierarchy and activities come from debriefings of Iraqi intelligence officials, interrogations of captured al Qaeda fighters, telephone intercepts, human intelligence, and satellite imagery.

Among the senior-most leaders of Ansar al Islam are three men who were responsible for keeping al Qaeda and Iraqi intelligence informed and happy: Mullah Krekar, Abu Wael, and Abu Musab al Zarqawi. Krekar is an eccentric religious authority who lived much of the last decade in Norway. Abu Wael is a lawyer by training who has for several years worked for Saddam's feared intelligence service as an outreach coordinator of sorts to a wide variety of radical Islamic groups. Al Zarqawi, something of an Ansar add-on, gained international prominence when Colin Powell cited him as a chief link between Iraq and al Qaeda during his presentation at the United Nations.

Together these men form the nucleus of an organization responsible for dozens of prewar attacks on pro-American Kurds and postwar attacks on coalition forces. Their brand of terror—combining the radical and the secular, rogue states and loose terrorist networks—is on a small scale precisely what American politicians from both parties had warned about for a decade.

Since the end of the Gulf War, a large swath of northeastern Iraq has been outside the direct control of the Iraqi regime. British and American fighter jets flew regular missions over the "no-fly" zone, closely monitoring Iraqi Army positions and regularly dodging antiaircraft fire from Saddam's troops. Iraqis living in the region, overwhelmingly of Kurdish extraction, were governed autonomously by two rival Kurdish political parties, the Patriotic Union of Kurdistan and the Kurdish Democratic Party.

Life in the north—frequently referred to as Iraqi Kurdistan—was good compared to life in the rest of Iraq. Kurds started small businesses, ran supermarkets and Internet cafés, and for the most part enjoyed a much higher standard of living than their countrymen to the south. Much of the terrain in Iraqi Kurdistan bears little resemblance to the flat, sweeping deserts throughout the rest of Iraq. The north is mountainous and, in parts, green and heavily forested. In other parts, including an area held by Ansar al Islam known as "Little Tora Bora," the barren, rocky landscape is reminiscent of Afghanistan.

Factional infighting was not uncommon, and the rivalry between the two Kurdish parties was often tense and sometimes deadly. When they weren't fighting each other, the *peshmerga* militias from the PUK and KDP fought a low-level war against Islamic radicals from neighboring villages.

All three Kurdish factions opposed the regime in Baghdad.

With the possible exception of the Marsh Arabs in southern Iraq, no one suffered from Saddam's brutality more than the Kurds. The world has been reminded again and again—but never enough—of the 1988 massacre in the Kurdish village of Halabja, in which Saddam's forces used chemical weapons on the village and slaughtered more than five thousand civilians. Other mass exterminations were not uncommon, though less publicized. In 1991, when the Kurds rose up against the regime at President George H. W. Bush's urging, Saddam violently crushed the rebellion, spilling the blood of thousands of Kurds.

Despite this, one Kurdish faction or another occasionally collaborated with the regime for its own immediate political advantage. The KDP, led by Massoud Barzani, accepted the decisive help of the Iraqi regime in 1996 in its hostilities against the PUK. And years later, with the founding of Ansar al Islam, Kurdish Islamists—or at least their leaders—decided it was in their interests to deal with Saddam.

According to U.S. and Kurdish intelligence officials, it was no coincidence that Jund al Islam, the precursor to Ansar, was established ten days before the attacks in America on September 11, 2001. Al Qaeda leaders anticipated being driven from Afghanistan after the attacks and sought an alternative base of operations. Bin Laden had enjoyed good relations with Kurdish extremists for years. The relationship between al Qaeda and its like-minded Kurdish brethren was constantly evolving, but intensified in 1999 when bin Laden began to establish terrorist training camps in Iraqi Kurdistan. One of these camps was reportedly operational by the end of that year. According to several al Qaeda detainees, bin Laden sent word to his allies in

Iraqi Kurdistan shortly before the September 11 attacks that the time had come for them to unite.

U.S. intelligence officials say they do not know whether Saddam's regime helped bin Laden and his Kurdish sympathizers construct the camps, but they have obtained reporting that in 2000 a senior Iraqi intelligence agent working with Ansar al Islam offered al Qaeda "safe haven" in northeastern Iraq. Reports indicate that bin Laden, in his communications with the Iraqi regime over the years, had consistently requested terrorist training facilities in Iraq—including Iraqi Kurdistan. And Iraqi Kurdish terrorists had been frequent visitors to bin Laden's camps in Afghanistan.

The first detailed reports about Ansar al Islam came not from U.S. intelligence but from a groundbreaking report in *The New Yorker* magazine, the same story that established Zawahiri's 1992 trip to Baghdad. Jeffrey Goldberg, in northern Iraq to report a story about the Iraqi regime's repression of the Kurds, was given access to several prisoners at a Kurdish jail in Sulaimaniya. The Kurds had been trying for months to convince the CIA to visit the facility and interrogate the detainees, who were being held for their role in attacks against Kurdish interests. According to the Kurds, the CIA had been unresponsive.

Goldberg's exhaustively reported piece was peppered with caveats. "The Kurds have an obvious interest in lining up on the American side in the war against terror," he wrote. "But the officials did not, as far as I know, compel anyone to speak to me, and I did not get the sense that allegations made by prisoners were shaped by their captors."

The prisoners' claims were sensational:

The allegations include charges that Ansar al Islam has received funds directly from al Qaeda; that the intelligence service of Saddam Hussein has joint control, with al Qaeda operatives, over Ansar al Islam; that Saddam Hussein hosted a senior leader of al Qaeda in Baghdad in 1992; that a number of al Qaeda members fleeing Afghanistan have been secretly brought into territory controlled by Ansar al Islam; and that Iraqi intelligence agents smuggled conventional weapons, and possibly even chemical and biological weapons, into Afghanistan. If these charges are true, it would mean that the relationship between Saddam's regime and al Qaeda is far closer than previously thought.

Indeed it was. Goldberg interviewed Qassem Hussein Mohammed, a twenty-year veteran of the Mukhabarat from Basra, Iraq's second largest city. Qassem was arrested by Kurdish forces shortly before he reached the northern Iraqi town of Biyara. He told Goldberg that he had been dispatched to the north by Iraqi intelligence to find an intelligence agent named Abu Wael. Qassem's bosses with the Mukhabarat had received a report that Abu Wael had been captured by American forces in northern Iraq, and they were worried, perhaps, that Abu Wael would disclose his dual role as a Mukhabarat agent and a leader of Ansar al Islam. Qassem spoke openly about Abu Wael: "He's an employee of the Mukhabarat. He's the actual decision-maker in the group"—Ansar al Islam—"but he's an employee of the Mukhabarat."

Goldberg also interviewed an Iraqi named Haqi Ismail. According to Kurdish intelligence officials, his family had long-standing ties to Iraqi intelligence; his uncle had been the top

Mukhabarat officer in southern Iraq. Ismail admitted to training in an al Qaeda camp in Afghanistan, after which he took a job in the Taliban Foreign Ministry. When asked directly whether he was employed by Iraqi intelligence, he demurred. "I prefer not to talk about that."

Goldberg's account was corroborated in July 2003 by a documentary team from Britain working for PBS's *Wide Angle*. The program aired videotaped interviews with prisoners making similar allegations.

The CIA, however, was still reluctant to interview the prisoners, preferring to base its analysis of Ansar al Islam on satellite photographs and communications intercepts. That effort paid some dividends. A top-secret report in May 2002 "claimed that an Iraqi intelligence official, praising Ansar al Islam, provided it with $100,000 and agreed to continue to give assistance."

In the weeks after the September 11 attacks, U.S. intelligence tracked the movement of a significant number of al Qaeda and Taliban fighters to northern Iraq. On August 3, 2002, a CIA senior executive intelligence briefing summarized in the Feith memo noted that reports of al Qaeda regrouping in Iraq "are consistent with satellite imagery showing increased activity since last fall near a facility in Sargat, near Khurmal, at which al Qaeda associates and Ansar al Islam may be producing lethal toxins."

But the CIA never sent anyone to check out these reports. In a September 10, 2002, article on the front page of the *Washington Post*, Dana Priest reported that intelligence analysts "concluded they cannot validate" reports of "links between Hussein and al Qaeda members who have taken refuge in northern Iraq." Several paragraphs later, readers learned why. "One senior counterterrorism official confirmed that the CIA knew of the detentions and that U.S. officials have not interrogated the prisoners. 'We really don't know whether they are under al Qaeda or Saddam's control,' the official said. 'Ansar trained in Afghan camps. They used Afghanistan as their headquarters. It's tough to nail down the other details. It's not implausible that they are working with Saddam. His intel links into northern Iraq are very strong.'"

Six months after Goldberg's report, and just one month before Congress would vote to authorize war in Iraq, the CIA had not sent anyone to interrogate prisoners claiming detailed knowledge of collaboration between Saddam Hussein and Osama bin Laden. It was a staggering oversight that infuriated Bush administration policy makers.

When the CIA finally interrogated the prisoners in fall 2002, their initial assessments were mixed. One prisoner gave a detailed description of the Ansar camps—information that the CIA was able to corroborate by comparing it to satellite photos and new reporting about the group. He was deemed highly credible. But when the same prisoner offered a similarly detailed account of the Mukhabarat's involvement in Ansar al Islam, CIA interrogators decided that his story was less credible. According to a Bush administration official skeptical of that analysis, the CIA reported that Qassem's body language throughout the second portion of the interview suggested he was less certain of the information on the Iraqi connection.

The CIA reported in December 2002 that Ansar extremists had obtained VX nerve gas from the Iraqi regime. The report was first disclosed by Barton Gellman in the *Washington Post* on

December 12: "The Bush administration has received a credible report that Islamic extremists affiliated with al Qaeda took possession of a chemical weapon in Iraq last month or late in October, according to two officials with firsthand knowledge of the report and its source. They said government analysts suspect that the transaction involved the nerve agent VX and that a courier managed to smuggle it overland through Turkey." The CIA report came from a "sensitive and credible" source and was included in the most urgent threat analyses.

At the same time, the agency was learning more about the activities of Abu Musab al Zarqawi. For years, al Zarqawi ran a terrorist organization known as al Tawhid, which had focused its efforts on unsettling the government in Jordan. Based on information obtained from debriefings of senior al Qaeda operatives, U.S. intelligence officials believe al Zarqawi moved back to Afghanistan in 2000 and assumed control of a terrorist training camp specializing in poisons.

Al Zarqawi and bin Laden lieutenant Abu Zubaydah were wanted in connection with a foiled plot to blow up a Radisson SAS hotel in Amman, Jordan, in December 1999. According to a senior Bush administration official, Zubaydah, captured in Pakistan on March 28, 2002, identified al Zarqawi in one of his first debriefings as "one of the main people within bin Laden's circle who wanted to work with the Iraqis."

He would later be proved right. After sustaining a serious injury to his leg during the war in Afghanistan, al Zarqawi traveled to Iraq in late May 2002. According to Colin Powell's February 5, 2003, presentation to the UN Security Council, al Zarqawi went to Baghdad for medical treatment, "staying in the capital of Iraq for two months while he recuperated to fight another day." A foreign intelligence service that had been closely tracking al Zarqawi's movements, Powell said, "assessed that al Zarqawi entered Iraq with Iraqi intelligence knowledge and that Iraqi intelligence knows his location and plans to use his network to retaliate for attacks on Iraq."

After al Zarqawi's arrival in Baghdad, the United States twice communicated with the Iraqi regime, with Jordan as the intermediary. According to Powell, the U.S. government "passed details that should have made it easy to find Zarqawi." Iraqis claimed to have no knowledge of his whereabouts. The omnipresence of Iraqi intelligence made those denials hard to believe. So, too, does a detail Powell didn't mention because U.S. intelligence officials did not yet know it.

Al Zarqawi didn't check into just any Baghdad medical facility; his leg was amputated and he was fitted for a prosthetic limb at the city's best hospital. Average Iraqis, to say nothing of al Qaeda terrorists, were unlikely walk-ins. The Olympic Hospital treated Baghdad's elite, including many high-ranking regime officials. The hospital's director was Saddam's eldest son, Uday Hussein.

During al Zarqawi's convalescence, according to Powell, "nearly two dozen extremists converged on Baghdad and established a base of operations there." These al Qaeda affiliates based in Baghdad coordinated "the movement of people, money, and supplies into and throughout Iraq for his network." At the time of Powell's speech, they had been "operating freely in the Iraqi capital for eight months."

While many in the establishment media were impressed with Powell's presentation, particularly the long section on Iraq's possession of WMD, journalists remained skeptical of

Iraq's connections with al Qaeda. On ABC's *World News Tonight* just hours after the testimony, investigative reporter Brian Ross raised questions about Powell's claims of Iraqi links to Ansar al Islam.

As Ross showed video of Powell's presentation, a graphic that read "Weak Link?" flashed on the screen.

"There's no doubt Ansar al Islam is a radical Islamic terror group," Ross said. "Their own videos show it. Their ties to al Qaeda are also well documented. But they operate in a part of Iraq not controlled by Saddam Hussein and their leaders say they seek to overthrow Saddam Hussein and his government."

The piece cut to Mullah Krekar, Ansar's longtime leader and religious authority, then living openly in Norway. "[The Iraqi leaders] are our enemy," Krekar said. "Really, they are also our enemy." Krekar also said he had no association with al Zarqawi. Ross noted that British intelligence was skeptical of the links: "another blow to the U.S. case."

But the most interesting information from the ABC interview with Mullah Krekar never saw the air. Krekar explained that the aim of Ansar al Islam is to "overthrow the Iraqi regime and replace it with an Islamic state." He was asked whether he knew Abu Wael, Ansar al Islam's third-ranking official, who also reportedly worked for Iraqi intelligence. "I know Abu Wael for 25 years," said Krekar. "And he is in Baghdad. And he is an Arabic member of our *shura*, our leadership council also."

He is in Baghdad. That revelation, if true, was almost certainly unintentional. By Krekar's telling, Abu Wael was in the leadership of a group that existed to overthrow Saddam. Taking Krekar at face value, it is theoretically possible that Abu

Wael was in Baghdad as part of that effort, and that such a high-level opponent of the regime had somehow slipped past a vigilant Iraqi Intelligence Service on high alert six weeks before the war. But the question remains: why would Krekar broadcast that fact in a television interview?

Given the numerous corroborated accounts of Abu Wael's involvement with Iraqi intelligence, the more likely scenario is that Abu Wael was in Baghdad because the regime—his employer—wanted him there.

Another prisoner, Ansar member Rebwar Mohammed Abdul, later told a reporter from the *Los Angeles Times* that he had heard about Abu Wael directly from Mullah Krekar. Abdul said he had no personal knowledge of Saddam–al Qaeda links, but mentioned an interesting detail. "I never talked to Wael, but I saw him three times in meetings with Mullah Krekar. The mullah told us that Wael was a friend of his for 23 years and that they had met in Baghdad while Wael was an intelligence officer."

Two days after Powell's presentation, a story in the *Washington Post* questioned the connection between Iraq and Abu Musab al Zarqawi that had been the focus of the Iraq–al Qaeda section of the report. "Several experts described Powell's presentation as very strong in public relations terms," wrote Walter Pincus on February 7, 2003, in an article headlined "Alleged al Qaeda Ties Questioned." These experts "questioned the details of his description of the Zarqawi group and its relationship with Baghdad."

Democrats on the Senate Armed Services Committee, seizing on the article, grilled CIA director Tenet in an appearance he made before the panel five days later, on February 12, 2003.

The testimony came a month before the Iraq War. Tenet refused to budge: "He is a senior al Qaeda associate who has met with bin Laden, who has received money from al Qaeda leadership, and on my list of top 30 individuals that are required to decapitate and denigrate this organization, Mr. Zarqawi's on that list. The fact [is] that he is a contract [terrorist] where he does things on his own—but he has an intimate relationship with him and we classify him as a senior al Qaeda associate well known to all of them."

European officials had arrested dozens of terrorists connected to al Zarqawi in the months before Powell's testimony. In London, a British police officer was killed after authorities broke up a al Zarqawi–sponsored cell manufacturing the toxic substance ricin. And Powell had blamed al Zarqawi associates for the assassination of Laurence Foley, a State Department employee in Jordan.

But Democrats on the intelligence committee remained unconvinced. Tenet, undeterred, said it was "inconceivable" that al Zarqawi and his two dozen associates were in Baghdad without the knowledge of the Iraqi regime. He expanded on that comment in a heated exchange with Senator Ted Kennedy.

Sir, let me just take a few minutes because you raised a number of important points. Let me put this poisons and gas thing in some context because aren't—there are 116 people in jail in France, in Spain, in Italy, and in Great Britain who received training and guidance out of a network run by an individual who is sitting in Baghdad today and supported by two dozen of his associates.

Now, that is something important for the American people to also understand. Iraq has provided a safe haven in a permissive environment for these people to operate. And the other things that are very compelling to us are—just so I can close the loop on this issue is—we also know from very reliable information that there's been some transfers, training in chemical and biologicals from the Iraqis to al Qaeda. So we're already in this mix in a way that's very, very important for us to worry about how far it goes . . .

The CIA continued to collect information on al Zarqawi. Two weeks after Tenet's testimony, a CIA senior executive memorandum on February 21, 2003, later summarized in the Feith memo, went even further. "Close al Qaeda associate al Zarqawi has had an operational alliance with Iraqi officials. As of October 2002, al Zarqawi maintained contacts with the IIS to procure weapons and explosives, including surface-to-air missiles from an IIS officer in Baghdad." The memo continues: "Zarqawi was setting up sleeper cells in Baghdad to be activated in case of a U.S. occupation of the city, suggesting his operational cooperation with the Iraqis may have deepened in recent months. Such cooperation could include IIS provision of secure operating bases and steady access to arms and explosives in preparation for a possible U.S. invasion."

By the time the war began, the Iraqi regime boasted that it had recruited four thousand jihad fighters, although U.S. military officials put the figure closer to two thousand. Ansar al Islam, which coordinated the movements of many of these fighters, took on new importance. Although most of the resistance in southern Iraq came from Iraqi Army regulars and members of Saddam's elite fighting unit Fedayeen Saddam, British soldiers told reporters that Iraqi detainees reported fighting alongside al Qaeda militants in Az Zubayr, outside Basra. And coalition troops regularly reported finding foreign passports on dead combatants throughout Iraq. Some of these passports had Iraqi visas, issued in the months before the war. One foreign fighter listed "jihad" as the reason for his travels.

As coalition bombing raids began in Iraqi Kurdistan, many Ansar fighters—most of them non-Iraqis—were killed. Others fled, traveling primarily south and east. The Ansar al Islam leadership announced their repositioning in a statement posted on the Internet on March 31, 2003. "Our bases in northern Iraq were completely evacuated Thursday night and the mujahedin, with all their weapons, have redeployed to new positions better suited for the coming battles."

Rank-and-file fighters were dispatched south to fill in the cells that al Zarqawi and his associates had set up before the war. But as many as three hundred of Ansar al Islam's top leaders, including al Zarqawi and Abu Wael, escaped over the border into Iran. Ansar fighters now in captivity say these leaders had help from Iranian immigration officials.

The Ansar camps were annihilated in the first days of the war. Among the debris were several hundred passports belonging to suspected Ansar and al Qaeda fighters, dozens of them bearing visas issued by the Iraqi regime. U.S. Special Forces soldiers found copies of al Qaeda's *Encyclopedia of Jihad,* computer disks filled with fundamentalist religious teachings, and lists of al Qaeda terrorists scattered throughout Europe and North America. They also discovered suicide belts, recipes for various poisons, and weapons identical to those provided to the Iraqi Army.

The evidence that Saddam supported Ansar al Islam grew stronger when Kurdish authorities captured Abdul Rahman al Shamari, who claimed he was a Mukhabarat agent from 1997 to 2002. Jonathan Schanzer, an Arabic-speaking terrorism expert, interviewed al Shamari in February 2004 as he was researching a forthcoming book on al Qaeda affiliate groups such as Ansar al Islam.

Al Shamari admitted that his division of the Mukhabarat provided Ansar with weapons—"mostly mortar rounds"—and financing. "On one occasion we gave them ten million Swiss dinars," al Shamari said, referring to the currency in Iraq before 1990. The payment, about $700,000, was one of many from Iraqi intelligence to Ansar, with additional funding coming "every month or two," according to al Shamari.

Schanzer showed the prisoner a photograph of a man in traditional Islamic dress with a long gray beard. Al Shamari identified the man as Colonel Saadan Mahmoud Abdul Latif al Aani, whose nom de guerre is Abu Wael. The picture was old, the prisoner said, as Abu Wael's long salt-and-pepper beard had grown completely white.

Al Shamari said that Saddam had instructed Abu Wael to recruit Ansar fighters from radical Islamic groups throughout the Middle East. He recalled in great detail Abu Wael's liaison with bin Laden–affiliated terrorist groups in Egypt, Jordan, Lebanon, Syria, Turkey, and Yemen. Fighters were given Iraqi visas and trained in Iraq, with some of them receiving instruction at the Salman Pak terrorist training facility. Abu Wael distributed Saddam's money to these groups, sometimes with the help of Abu Musab al Zarqawi—the one-legged terrorist who starred in Powell's testimony.

Al Shamari said that three months before the invasion of Iraq, a sign on the wall of the Mukhabarat headquarters indicated that there was a 75 percent chance of a U.S. invasion. He described an agreement between al Zarqawi; the Mukhabarat; and the head of all Iraqi security services, Qusay Hussein: if the United States strikes the Ansar camps near Biyara in Iraqi Kurdistan, Ansar fighters would "go south." Al Shamari said three separate times in the forty-five-minute interview that Qusay Hussein was intimately involved in the planning of Ansar al Islam operations.

Many of al Shamari's allegations have been corroborated by a senior Ansar al Islam terrorist who, according to Kurdish sources, had never met the Iraqi intelligence official. The Ansar fighter, who goes by the name Qods, also described the plan to send Ansar al Islam south when the war began.

Qods traveled with Ansar leaders to Ravansar, Iran, shortly after hostilities commenced. He remained there with Abu Wael and Abu Musab al Zarqawi until May, when he says he was dispatched to Baghdad. Abu Wael told Qods to meet Abu Wael's son, Omar, at a safe house in Baghdad. The message was simple: "We're in Iran. We're ready to come back if you're ready to help."

Qods conveyed the message to Omar in Baghdad and returned to Iran with a response: "I can take 40 or 50 people. I want the leadership to come back." Qods, who claims to be Ansar's tenth highest-ranking official, says he knew nothing about the support Ansar was receiving from the Iraqi regime until he was elevated to Ansar's leadership. He voiced his objections to other Ansar members, and the differences led to a falling-out—with Qods and another Kurdish Ansar leader named Abu Hamid on one side, and the Arab leadership on the other.

U.S. military and coalition leaders alternately talked up and played down the role of foreign fighters in postwar resistance—sometimes in the same briefings. At a mid-October 2003 Pentagon briefing, military officials put the number of foreign fighters at three thousand. One week later, a "senior military intelligence officer" briefing reporters at coalition headquarters in Baghdad suggested that number was high. "The foreign fighter piece of this is very small," he said. "We're talking hundreds." Days later, Major General Ray Odierno, whose Fourth Infantry Division troops were responsible for the so-called Sunni Triangle, said his forces "have not seen any al Qaeda yet." He put the number of foreign fighters at "2, 3, 4, 5 percent."

What is indisputable, however, is that the spike in deadly attacks bearing al Qaeda hallmarks—chiefly suicide attacks and truck bombings—coincided with the return of Ansar leaders to Iraq in early summer 2003. U.S. officials believe that Ansar and its affiliated groups throughout Iraq are responsible for the bombing of UN headquarters in Baghdad and a Shiite mosque in Najaf in August 2003. A letter intercepted by Kurdish officials and passed to the U.S. military claims involvement in twenty-five postwar bombings, and U.S. officials say they are certain that the letter was authored by al Zarqawi.

Barham Salih, prime minister of the Kurdish Regional Government in Sulaimaniya, knows the lethality of Ansar al Islam firsthand. In April 2002, five of his bodyguards died when Ansar fighters tried unsuccessfully to assassinate him. Salih, a soft-spoken intellectual who speaks in carefully chosen terms, becomes animated when asked about the notion, articulated most often by Senate Democrats and other opponents of the Iraq War, that Saddam would not support Islamic radicals in Kurdistan. "Bullshit," he says. "Yes, they hate each other, but they're very utilitarian. Saddam Hussein, a secular infidel to many jihadists, had no problem giving money to Hamas. This debate [about whether Saddam worked with al Qaeda] is stupid. The proof is there."

Kurdish intelligence sources believe that the Iraqi regime supported Kurdish Islamic extremists for years. "It's strictly utilitarian—they had no problem working together to take on the Big Evil and their [Kurdish] surrogates," says Salih. "This was not a marriage of convenience that came about after the war."

CHAPTER TWELVE

SEE NO EVIL

Iraqi intelligence documents from 1992 list Osama bin Laden as an Iraqi intelligence asset. Numerous sources have reported a 1993 nonaggression pact between Iraq and al Qaeda. The former deputy director of Iraqi intelligence now in U.S. custody says that bin Laden asked the Iraqi regime for arms and training in a face-to-face meeting in 1994. Senior al Qaeda leader Abu Hajer al Iraqi met with Iraqi intelligence officials in 1995. The National Security Agency intercepted telephone conversations between al Qaeda–supported Sudanese military officials and the head of Iraq's chemical weapons program in 1996. Al Qaeda sent Abu Abdallah al Iraqi to Iraq for help with weapons of mass destruction in 1997. An indictment from the Clinton-era Justice Department cited Iraqi assistance on al Qaeda "weapons development" in 1998. A senior Clinton administration counterterrorism official told the *Washington Post* that the U.S. government was "sure" Iraq had supported al Qaeda chemical weapons programs in 1999. An Iraqi working closely with the Iraqi embassy in Kuala Lumpur was photographed with September 11 hijacker Khalid al Mihdhar en route to a planning meeting for the bombing of the USS *Cole* and the

September 11 attacks in 2000. Satellite photographs showed al Qaeda members in 2001 traveling en masse to a compound in northern Iraq financed, in part, by the Iraqi regime. Abu Musab al Zarqawi, senior al Qaeda associate, operated openly in Baghdad and received medical attention at a regime-supported hospital in 2002. Documents discovered in postwar Iraq in 2003 reveal that Saddam's regime harbored and supported Abdul Rahman Yasin, an Iraqi who mixed the chemicals for the 1993 World Trade Center attack—the first al Qaeda attack on U.S. soil.

Then, on March 21, 2004, Richard Clarke, a former top counterterrorism official with access to all of this information, made a stunning declaration: "There's absolutely no evidence that Iraq was supporting al Qaeda, ever."

Clarke may find the evidence unpersuasive or may know of additional information that mitigates its importance. But that is not his claim. The evidence, he insists, does not exist. Why would Clarke say something so demonstrably false?

"If Iraq was involved with al Qaeda, whether they were involved with 9/11 or not, the whole counterterrorism policy of the 1990s was a failure," says a senior Bush administration official.

It's a good point, but one of many that Bush administration officials have been reluctant to make. Indeed, one of the most puzzling aspects of the debate about the Iraq–al Qaeda connection has been the unwillingness of the Bush administration to talk about it on the record. By all accounts, the evidence of the relationship has only strengthened since the end of combat in Iraq. But, stung by the controversy over President

Bush's reference, in his 2003 State of the Union address, to Iraq's alleged pursuit of uranium in Africa, and ever mindful of the current "gotcha" mentality of the establishment press, the White House is reluctant to make public any information that it deems even potentially controversial.

So in spring 2004, the White House adopted a new policy that would preclude public disclosure of Iraq–al Qaeda intelligence without the unanimous approval of U.S. intelligence agencies, guidelines that give skeptics at the CIA an effective veto over the release of new information. Still, in an interview in mid-March, radio talk show host Scott Hennen pressed national security adviser Condoleezza Rice about the administration's reluctance to talk more about Iraqi support for Islamic extremists and al Qaeda. "We will do that," she promised.

Among the items the administration might discuss is an Iraqi intelligence document recovered in postwar Iraq and in possession of the Defense Intelligence Agency. The DIA calls it a report of "contact between an IIS agent and Osama bin Laden in Syria." The meeting took place in March 1992, just weeks before bin Laden's name was included in another IIS document—the one first reported by *60 Minutes* and ignored by the establishment press—as an Iraqi intelligence asset in contact with IIS agents stationed in Syria.

Investigators from the FBI and DIA are using the second document, a twenty-page list of Iraqi intelligence assets in Kuwait and Saudi Arabia, to learn more about those involved in the 1993 assassination attempt on President George H. W. Bush in Kuwait. And in what could be a very interesting development, that document has also triggered a preliminary investigation into possible Iraqi intelligence involvement in the Khobar Towers bombings on June 25, 1996. "Alleged conspirators employed by IIS are wanted in connection with the Khobar Towers bombing and the assassination attempt in 1993 of former President Bush," reads a DIA summary of the findings. Previous investigations of the Khobar attacks have suggested that they were conducted by Iran, Hezbollah, or al Qaeda—or a combination of the three.

One of the most intriguing but frustrating developments in the limited investigation into Iraq-al Qaeda connections concerns an internal Iraqi intelligence memo. The document has frustrated DIA investigators because it is undated, but its contents are potentially quite significant. According to a DIA summary of the document, Iraqi intelligence officials held a planning session to discuss upcoming meetings between "UBL [Usama bin Laden], a Taliban representative, and the IIS." (The allusion to a Taliban representative suggests the meeting took place at some point after 1995, when the Taliban came to power in Afghanistan.) Discussions at the meetings were to focus on "attacking American targets."

U.S. officials cannot confirm that the meeting took place.

Former and current intelligence analysts and public officials often cite such inconclusive reporting as the basis for their skepticism of Iraq-al Qaeda connections. In many cases, their doubts reflect genuine differences about the quality of intelligence and the nature of the threat.

But some of the most outspoken critics, emboldened by the Bush administration's defensive posture, seem more interested in defending their earlier analyses and scoring political points. To do so, they shamelessly change their arguments when the facts no longer support their line of attack and make statements that directly contradict things they have said publicly before.

Richard Clarke has done both. Clarke was the official mentioned above who told the *Washington Post* that the U.S. government was "sure" Iraq was behind the VX precursor produced at the al Shifa factory destroyed in response to the 1998 al Qaeda attacks on U.S. embassies in Africa.

"Clarke said U.S. intelligence does not know how much of the substance was produced at al Shifa or what happened to it," wrote *Post* reporter Vernon Loeb, in an article published January 23, 1999. "But he said that intelligence exists linking bin Laden to al Shifa's current and past operators, the Iraqi nerve gas experts, and the National Islamic Front in Sudan."

With the possible exception of Senator Ted Kennedy, no one in Congress has been as fierce in his criticism of the Bush administration and its case for the war as Senator Carl Levin, a Democrat from Michigan who serves as vice chair of the Senate Armed Services Committee and is a senior member of the Senate Intelligence Committee. Levin has focused much of his critique on the connection between Iraq and al Qaeda and has repeatedly suggested that intelligence about the relationship was exaggerated. He made this point on November 9, 2003, in an appearance on *Fox News Sunday*.

"Did we know, for instance, with certainty that there was any relationship between the Iraqis and the terrorists that were in Afghanistan, bin Laden? The administration said that there's a connection between those terrorist groups in Afghanistan and Iraq. Was there a basis for that?"

There was, of course, and Levin surely knew it. His comments came two weeks after the intelligence committee had received the sixteen-page Feith memo on Iraq and al Qaeda collaboration. Even if he had doubts about the information in that document, much of which came from the CIA, Levin had been privy to more than a year's worth of testimony—written and oral, classified and open—from CIA director George Tenet and others detailing the on-again, off-again relationship between Iraqi intelligence and al Qaeda.

In the weeks after the war, Levin's criticism focused on the intelligence community, which, he said, had hyped the relationship between Iraq and al Qaeda.

"There is some evidence that there was an exaggeration by the intelligence community about that relationship," he said in an appearance on CNN on July 8, 2003. "We need them to be credible. That means no exaggeration. That means they have to give the unvarnished facts to the policy makers."

Those comments were an expansion of a similar argument Levin had made in a June 16, 2003, appearance on *The NewsHour with Jim Lehrer:* "We were told by the intelligence community that there was a very strong link between al Qaeda and Iraq."

But by February 2004, Levin was saying just the opposite.

"The intel didn't say that there is a direct connection between al Qaeda and Iraq," he told John Gibson of Fox News. "That was not the intel. That's what this administration exaggerated to produce. And so there are many instances where the administration went beyond the intelligence. . . . I'm saying that the administration's statements were exaggerations of what was given to them by the analysts and the intelligence community."

What had changed? Levin's early comments came as Bush administration officials were under fire for allegedly pressuring the intelligence analysts to produce reporting that would support its policy of regime change in Iraq. Months later, chief weapons inspector David Kay testified that he had seen no evidence of such pressure, a judgment confirmed by an exhaustive congressional investigation. Deprived of this talking point, Levin simply shifted his blame from the intelligence community to the Bush administration.

No Democrat was as disingenuous as Wesley Clark. "Certainly there's a connection between Iraq and al Qaeda," said Clark in October 2002, before he announced his decision to run for president. But as a candidate, Clark said, "there's no connection on that." He frequently cited the alleged Iraq–al Qaeda ties as evidence that the Bush administration had lied about the threat from Iraq.

While Wesley Clark, Richard Clarke, and top Clinton administration officials abandon their previous assessments of Iraq–al Qaeda collaboration and some Democratic politicians dismiss the connection, assigning blame wherever it suits their purposes, other experts defend their earlier analyses by arguing that the evidence of a relationship is not evidence of a threat.

The following exchange came during testimony in front of the September 11 commission on July 9, 2003. A commission member, former Secretary of the Navy John Lehman, raised the Iraq–al Qaeda issue with Judith Yaphe, a veteran CIA Iraq expert. Yaphe spoke of the "unwillingness of Saddam and Osama to consider cooperation" and testified that while the

Iraqi regime used Islamic extremists, it used only those groups it could control. So she did not think Saddam would work with al Qaeda. "I think he saw him as a threat, Osama as a threat, rather than a potential partner."

LEHMAN: There have been many press reports of the recovery of materials in Afghanistan and in Baghdad that indicate that al Qaeda received technical training in weapons of mass destruction, and received not only training but some ability to manufacture some of them. If—have you seen such evidence that the Iraqis are involved in this? And if not Iraqi intelligence, who?

YAPHE: No, I've seen the press reports just as you have. And frankly, I wouldn't be surprised if the Iraqis did provide some kind of training. That would be a perfectly normal thing—train them, see if you can suborn them, see if you can take them over—but that wouldn't mean that they trusted them or that they did operational planning. I think you have to be careful to sort out what you try to do to win hearts and minds of these groups to work for you and your objectives and where you draw the line. But again, I, as I say, that's almost what you expect to be part of the trade craft and the mission of the intelligence of these groups, and being in contact with or trying to win over and find out a lot about to penetrate these organizations. And we know that the Iraqis were highly successful in penetrating organizations that were opposed to them, the dissidents abroad, other terrorist groups—why wouldn't they have tried that with al Qaeda? I mean, what did they have to lose?

So even if Iraq provided al Qaeda training on weapons of mass destruction, the argument goes, it was only to penetrate an organization opposed to Saddam's regime. That might be an appropriate line for a CIA analyst or an academic, but it doesn't work for the policy makers who have to act upon suspected threats.

Although some Democrats have politicized the issue of the Iraq–al Qaeda connection, many others have not. And a few even backed the Bush administration. As noted, Hillary Clinton mentioned the al Qaeda presence in Baghdad in the speech she gave on October 10, 2002, announcing her intention to vote to authorize the use of force in Iraq.

Senator Joe Lieberman, a Democrat from Connecticut, was even more emphatic in an appearance on *Hardball* with Chris Matthews.

"I want to be real clear about the connection with terrorists. I've seen a lot of evidence on this. There are extensive contacts between Saddam Hussein's government and al Qaeda and other terrorist groups. I never could reach the conclusion that [Saddam] was part of September 11. Don't get me wrong about that. But there was so much smoke there that it made me worry. And you know, some people say with a great facility, al Qaeda and Saddam could never get together. He is secular and they're theological. But there's something that tied them together. It's their hatred of us."

Senator Evan Bayh, a Democrat from Indiana who sits on the intelligence committee, agrees. "Even if there's only a 10 percent chance that Saddam Hussein and Osama bin Laden would cooperate, the question is whether that's an acceptable level of risk. My answer to that would be an unequivocal *no*. We need to be much more pro-active on eliminating threats before they're imminent."

Bayh continues: "Some of the intelligence is strong, and some of it is murky. But that's the nature of intelligence on a relationship like this—lots of it is going to be speculation and conjecture. Following 9/11, we await certainty at our peril."

EPILOGUE

If policy makers and everyday American citizens are to accurately evaluate threats in the post–9/11 age, they must understand the risks posed by terrorists. There will—and should be—different views about what levels of risk require action. But, ultimately, policy makers must make difficult decisions, often based on imperfect information, about how and when to act to best protect the country.

The Bush administration tells us that the Iraq War was central to the Global War on Terror. Its critics call the Iraq War a distraction.

The disagreement is a fundamental one. The Bush administration advocates a policy of preemption that calls for targeting terrorists and the regimes that support them, with the goal of eliminating threats before they are imminent. Their opponents disagree.

The central question, then, is this: Would it have been possible to wage a serious Global War on Terror leaving the Iraqi regime of Saddam Hussein in power? To answer it, we must consider what we knew before September 11 and what we knew before the Iraq War.

As the campaign season heats up, the Bush administration is once again being criticized for failing to "connect the dots" that might have prevented the September 11 attacks. "I find it outrageous that the president is running for re-election on the grounds that he has done such great things about terrorism," said Richard Clarke on the March 21, 2004, edition of *60 Minutes*. "He ignored it. He ignored terrorism for months, when maybe we could have done something to stop 9/11. Maybe. We'll never know."

There were, we now know, multiple intelligence failures that left us vulnerable: terrorists who were not tracked, visas that were approved, memos that were ignored, telephone intercepts that were not translated. Those failures were the result of an intelligence bureaucracy that for systemic reasons didn't recognize the imminent threat. It is easy, in hindsight, to point out the errors and criticize those who committed them.

But the much-hyped evidence that the intelligence community had at its disposal in the summer before September 11 amounted to a smattering of isolated reports that suggested the coming attacks only if taken together and with a fair measure of imagination. In addition to a high level of intelligence "chatter," there was an internal FBI memo about suspicious activities at flight schools in Phoenix, a report out of Minnesota about a Middle Eastern man with a bizarre interest in airplanes, and unspecific CIA reporting about forthcoming al Qaeda attacks.

Policy makers at the White House and elsewhere in the national security hierarchy had even less information. One of the few sources available to policy makers and the public was a report on the psychology of terrorism published by the Congressional Research Service in 1999. On page 7 of the 178-page study was a passage about a possible al Qaeda attack in Washington, D.C. The prospective attack "could take several forms." In one scenario: "Suicide bombers belonging to al Qaeda's Martyrdom Battalion could crash-land an aircraft packed with high explosives (C-4 and semtex) into the Pentagon, the headquarters of the Central Intelligence Agency, or the White House."

Later, the report would receive worldwide attention as a specific warning of the threat that was realized on September 11. A network anchor wondered if it was possible that the White House had somehow missed it. A senator cited the report in his public call for an investigation into the 9/11 attacks. A journalist cited the report to the secretary of defense and raised a familiar question: "What did you know and when did you know it?" But at the time the study was released, it was a minor document in a wave of reporting on a topic discussed mostly in academic conferences and congressional committee meetings.

These were the dots that were never connected before September 11. There were but a few of them.

Contrast that with the knowledge available to policy makers prior to the Iraq War. The same report discussed above contained another stark warning, which appeared on the same page as the much-ballyhooed "forecast" of the al Qaeda attacks on Washington, D.C.: If "Iraq's Saddam Hussein decide[s] to use terrorists to attack the continental United States [he] would likely turn to bin Laden's al Qaeda. Al Qaeda is among the Islamic groups recruiting increasingly skilled professionals," including "Iraqi chemical weapons experts and others capable of helping to develop WMD. Al Qaeda poses the most serious terrorist threat to U.S. security interests, for al Qaeda's well-trained terrorists are actively engaged in a terrorist jihad against U.S. interests worldwide." This certainly fit neatly with what we already knew of Iraq. Saddam's regime harbored and supported notorious terrorists, including al Qaeda, until it fell on April 9, 2003. That regime trained and funded Islamic radicals, including al Qaeda, throughout the world for decades. The regime provided technology and arms to other rogue states and terrorist networks, including al Qaeda, even as the international community attempted to scrutinize its every action.

And these facts, like the reporting in this book, provide only a partial picture of Saddam Hussein's support for international terror and al Qaeda. In virtually all the reporting on the connection, one recurring point stands out: the intense desire of all parties to keep these relationships secret. The U.S. intelligence community now recognizes numerous high-level contacts between Iraq and al Qaeda; that these contacts are known despite concerted and sometimes elaborate efforts to conceal them suggests that there are many more. The same is true of arms shipments and financial transactions.

We are learning more every day in postwar Iraq. A year after the war ended, we have "a much clearer picture of collaboration," said one senior White House official.

The intelligence on the relationship between Iraq and al Qaeda available to President Bush and the Congress before the Iraq War was far more than simple dots waiting to be connected. The connection by then was well established. The only real question was what we would do about it.

Remnants of this connection fight side by side against Americans in the streets of Iraq. The battles will continue, probably for years, and the loss of life is saddening. But with Saddam Hussein in jail and Osama bin Laden probably hiding in a remote cave, we have already achieved a critical success in the Global War on Terror. The heart of the connection is no more.

ACKNOWLEDGMENTS

This book is the product of many people, most especially my sources. A good number of them must remain unnamed. I thank them for having the courage to talk to a reporter, again and again and often after considerable badgering, about an issue critically important to U.S. national security. This book is as much theirs as it is mine.

Bill Kristol and the editors and staff at the *Weekly Standard* have been helpful and patient as I focused my attention on this book. I am grateful to Richard Starr and Claudia Winkler for their editorial guidance as I reported on Iraq for the past two years, and especially to Fred Barnes for hiring me, three years ago.

I've come to know several other writers whose work on this subject greatly informed my own. They include Jeffrey Goldberg from *The New Yorker*, David Rose from *Vanity Fair*, and Jonathan Schanzer, who is at work on an al Qaeda book of his own. Michael Shapiro at Columbia University's Graduate School of Journalism and Ken Tomlinson, my longtime friend and mentor, provided valuable general advice.

Two researchers helped me with the book—Michael Goldfarb in Washington, D.C., and Katerina Zachovalova in

Prague, Czech Republic. Their work was professional and efficient, and the book is much better because of their contributions. The same is true of Johanna Stoberock, who put in long days and nights scrutinizing the open source facts that appear in the book.

Matt Labash, Tony Mecia, and Tim Townsend, excellent journalists all, proved themselves even better friends by slogging through early drafts of the manuscript and offering candid and insightful feedback. Their criticism was constructive and their occasional praise both surprising and encouraging.

The team at HarperCollins has been extraordinary. From Cathy Hemming and Susan Weinberg on down, their flexibility and professionalism has made this project an enjoyable one. David Hirshey's gentle insistence on seeing the big picture—the forest and the trees—made the book far more accessible than it otherwise would have been. A special thanks to Nick Trautwein, one of the most perceptive and discerning editors I have ever worked with. My agent, Eric Simonoff, stood with me even when I am certain that he thought I was nuts. His counsel has been invaluable.

I am especially grateful to my family for the support they've given me on this book and for my whole life. Grace Forester, my grandma, has been a constant inspiration. She has become quite the news junkie and regularly brings to my attention interesting developments that I've missed.

Finally, thanks to my wife, Carrie. She has for months put up with reams of research files and countless books strewn about the house, showing more patience than is required of any newlywed. Her patience and love are my greatest sources of encouragement.